CW01003713

THE FOODIE BOOK

For cooks and non-cooks,
by cooks and non-cooks.

in aid of cancer charities

Copyright © Catherine Broughton

The right of Catherine Broughton to be identified as the author of this work is confirmed in accordance with the Copyright, Designs & Patents Act 1988.

All rights reserved. No copy, reproduction or transmission of this work, or part of this work, to include the cover illustration, may be made without written permission from the author. Any person who does so may be liable to prosecution.

A CIP record catalogue of this book is available at the British Library

Published by Catherine Broughton via Amazon

The contents of this book have been collected from all over the world and in no way reflect any opinions, religions or any other controversial issue on any topic or at any level. They are for the sole purpose of creating a fund-raising book in aid of cancer research.

More about Catherine Broughton on
turquoisemoon.co.uk

More about ATLA Publishing on
atlapublishing.com

Table of contents

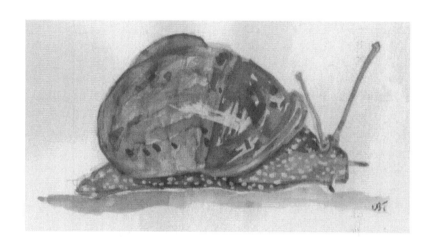

Introduction

By Guy Thair

"I have always loved food and I have been hooked on cooking since I was a child, (my mum died from a brain tumour when I was just 9, leaving me to take on extra responsibilities around the house) so I was delighted when Catherine Broughton asked me to introduce this new collection of recipes, and articles with a decidedly culinary flavour.

There is something special about a cookery book isn't there?
They have a certain cosy, reassuring warmth to them, one that makes us feel simultaneously domesticated and adventurous; as though we are starting out on a wondrous new journey, but one on which we will be accompanied by an old and trusted friend, who knows exactly what we like best.
So what could be better than a book that not only gives you a wealth of mouth-watering ideas and cooking tips, but also a selection of globetrotting anecdotes, funny stories and recipes from around the world, some serious and some with a not-so-serious twist?

Well, how about one which does all that, and raises money for cancer research at the same time?

Both Catherine and I have lost friends and family members to cancer recently and I'm willing to bet that most of you have been touched in some way by a disease that makes no distinction between young and old; sometimes robbing us of those whose lives have barely begun and sometimes bringing grief and loss into our lives when we thought that all we had was time, time to spend enjoying life with our loved ones in our autumn years.

So I was happy to contribute these few words, along with the others who have donated writing and illustrations, it's the very least I could do.

Because anything which can raise awareness and money to help combat this insidious disease, whilst giving pleasure and hope to those of us that it has affected, can only be a good thing.

I hope that by buying this book, you too will derive that unique feeling of satisfaction that comes from knowing you have helped save lives, at the same time as providing the ones you love with new and exciting tastes from around the world."

Guy Thair lives in Devon in the south west of the UK and has been writing his blog, Diary of an Internet Nobody, (under the pseudonym dalecooper57) for about three years. He only recently began experimenting with writing short fiction, taking most of his inspiration from writing prompts on other blogs.

diaryofaninternetnobody.com

RJP

Dedication

This book is dedicated to all those who work at the St Peter and St James Hospice in Lewes, Sussex, England, and to all those who have lost a loved one to cancer.

Dedication and title chosen by Pippa Taylor, Sussex.

From one of several St Peter & St James fund-raising shops:

'Simply Fashion' in Uckfield High Street is one of eight charity shops raising vital funds for St Peter and St James hospice. We specialise in women's and men's fashion and have a section of vintage clothing.

We maintain a high standard of quality and have designer clothing, high street brands handbags and shoes.

The shop is laid out to be bright and welcoming and is often mistaken for a boutique, not a charity shop. We receive compliments daily from our wonderful customers on the shop, some have said it's their favourite shop, or the best charity shop they've been to.

The lay-out is constantly changing to accommodate donations, occasion and season, with wonderful window displays done by my assistant manager or myself. We change the window display weekly, recent themes include 'by the pool', 'in the jungle', 'butterflies', garden tea party' and a massive rainbow made from over 40 coloured scarves.

We have a great team of volunteers, which without we could not run such a successful shop. They range from 16 to 76 and are dedicated and all a delight to work with.

Approximately once a year we have a fashion show in the shop which is a ticket only event and always a great success, vintage and modern outfits are modelled by staff and volunteers which guarantees a great evening!

Yours truly,

Delia Johnson shop manager.
Valerie Liddington assistant manager

This book is a fundraiser! Please tell your friends about it and share on your social media.

Merrill Plowman

"And when you crush an apple with your teeth, say to it in your heart:

Your seeds shall live in my body,
And the buds of your tomorrow shall blossom in my heart,
And your fragrance shall be my breath,
And together we shall rejoice through all the seasons."

— Kahlil Gibran

Contributors

Cover art by **Allison Hurden**:

I have had a passion for art from a very young age and studied at Weston college. I later did a foundation course and continued with short courses to fit in with the usual busy life. My natural instinct is to study the detail and enjoy constantly discovering new ideas and techniques.

www.alihurden.webeden.co.uk

Interior art work (initialled) by **Susan C Russell**:
Susan (SCR) enjoyed a career encompassing nursing and complementary therapies before moving to live in France, in 2012. Now, apart from running a gite with her husband, she enjoys the quiet country life that gives her time to indulge her love of drawing and creative writing.
suerussell@cantal-gite.com

Merrill Plowman:

Having studied A-level Botany at school, Merrill (MP) retained a strong interest in plants, became interested in Botanical illustration and on retirement took up the art of Botanical painting. She gained a distinction in the Society of Botanical Artists Distance Learning Diploma last year. She is a member of Nymans Florilegium Society and a founder member of the Botanical Art Society of Sussex(BASS).She has exhibited with BASS at Wakehurst Place and other venues and at Nymans National Trust property with Nymans Florilegium.

beehives@btinternet.com

Brian Thornton (BT):

Brian lives in a small ex mining village in South Wales. He studied Maths and Statistics at University but an artist friend told him that 'one can learn to draw'. Brian has had more time to practice since retiring and also plays guitar and keeps fit walking and cycling in the UK.

Stephen Roberts:

Steve Roberts (SR) is an Independent pencil artist specialising in celebrity portraits and custom designs from photographs. Contact him on Facebook: Special Portrait Reproductions.

Carol Morse:

@CarolScholes (Twitter) or Carol Scholes LinkedIn. Carol (CM) can also be contacted on Facebook. Carol is English and lives in Sussex.

Richard Pettit (RJP):

Richard is English and works with the Barnado's children's charity (barnardos.org.uk). He is also an artist:

richardpettittart.com

Catherine Broughton (CB):

Catherine is an author and has written several books available from Amazon or Barnes & Noble.

turquoisemoon.co.uk

Frances Black, Jean Simpkins, Sally Findlay, Philip Davies
All members of the Berry Lane Art Group. This Art Group run by Gillian Blair & Frances Black has been operating since 2009 & has over seventy members. Classes are run in Croxley Green Rickmansworth & Chorley Wood. For more information about these classes visit their web site berrylaneart.com or follow them on Facebook: Berry lane art group.

Mandy Broughton:
Art has been a passion for me all my life. I am best known for seascape paintings.   However, I enjoy painting other things such as food and people. My paintings are in the collections of people and corporations in England, France, South Africa, United Arab Emirates and the USA.
broughtonart.com
facebook.com/MandyBroughton
twitter.com/MandyBroughton1

Jenni Gayle:
Calling herself urbanduckxxo, Jenni can be contacted via Instagram, Facebook, DeviatArt and Tumblr

BT

Contributions, with many thanks, from:

Claire Divall, Anne Brewer, Vaughan's Kitchen/the Bistro in Devises, Pippa Taylor, Lucas Kane, Shelley Dootson-Greenland, Jan Cooper, Anja Eriksson, Lorraine Sodoba, Lucy Thorburn, Victor Rudez, Guy Thair, Olav Forsgren, Catherine Broughton, Toby Williams, Alix Taylor, Malek Montag, Sarah Bailey-Williams, Mireille Tomono, Charmayne Polsih, Alix Norman, Sheila Pinney, Nick Goodrich, Fatima Nazir, Louise Elson, Sally Carayon, Gilly P-T, The Very Round Café/tea rooms in Milwaukee, Gyuri Guti, Lesley Tumulty, Manie Larsson, Vivien Houghton, Bob Ranyard, Guilaine Vautrain, Rania M M Watts, Amanda Wren-Grimwood, John Holland, Alison Neale, Nicky Rodgers, Clare Brown, Ann Haycock, Susan Newell, Brian Thornton, Celine Jacques.

<u>These recipes and contributions come to us from:</u>

UK, USA, Tanzania, South Africa, Algeria, Denmark, France, Iceland, Poland, Croatia, Sweden, New Caledonia, Holland, Isreal, Australia, Switzerland and Hungary.

<u>Author's note.</u>

I have to be honest and tell you this was all vastly more trouble and work than I ever imagined ! At the outset it seemed simple enough – just collect recipes and drawings – and I thought it would take month or so. However, it has now been 5 months of persuading, talking, reminding, copying and pasting, correcting, re-arranging … and so on. Still, it is in a very good cause, a cause that touches us all, so I have been pleased to do it … and even more pleased to reach the end!

I do hope everybody will commit to at least buying one book and getting others to buy two or three more.

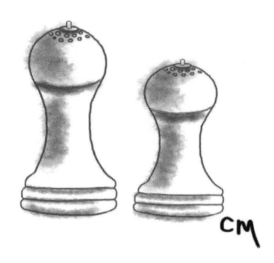

Recipes

OAT MILK

From Afan Arts in Wales

Wishing to reduce my cow`s milk intake, I now use my own oat milk on cereal for breakfast and in tea. It is delicious and a fraction of the price of shop bought oat milk which contains additives, emulsifiers etc. Oats contain soluble fibre and are recommended for heart health and to lower cholesterol.

1. Ingredients: 1cup of good quality rolled oats (I recommend organic UK oats), 5 cups of water, pinch salt, 1tsp dark brown sugar/ molasses.
2. Mix the oats with the water.
3. Add the salt and sugar and leave to soak in the fridge for some hours or overnight.
4. Blend and sieve.

Notes and variations:

Sieving is not necessary. The sediment will settle and can be stirred up before using to create extra `creaminess`. You can alter the number of cups of water added to suit your taste. Alternative sweeteners such as honey or dates may be used. Salt and sugar can be omitted entirely. If boiled, this will thicken, so is not recommended for a cappuccino! Can be used in cooking though, where this does not matter, eg pancakes.

The salt content is about the same as cow`s milk and the sugar content about a fifth of that of cow`s milk (although a different type of sugar).

In the rolling process, the oats are steamed slightly rendering them digestible, ie they are not raw.

BT

If an apple a day keeps the doctor away, what does an onion do?

Keeps everyone away!

EDIBLE BERRIES

Toby Williams (England)

Hairy bitter cress, stinging nettle, ramsons, hawthorn, goose grass, dandelion, bramble, blackthorn, spear thistle, ground ivy, primrose, larch (tea), yellow archangel, wood sorrel, broad-leaved plantain, silver weed, white dead nettle, red dead nettle, hedge garlic, marsh thistle, cherry and hog weed. Not bad for a little stroll!

rangerdays.co.uk

Music with dinner is an insult to both the chef and the violinist.

G.K.Chesterton

MAN-SANDWICH

Alix Taylor, Sussex

This is a sandwich created by Alix Taylor (age 15) for Big Hungry Men! You make the sandwich in the usual way, adding or reducing quantities to taste. This is a filling and energizing mid-day meal for men who work hard, and can be eaten hot or cold.

1. Tiger loaf bread, sliced in half lengthwise

2. 4 thin-ish steaks

3. Several rashers of bacon

4. Any spices to suit, or mango chutney, BBQ sauce

5. 4 tomatoes, sliced

6. 4 leaves of romaine lettuce

7. 1 lime

8. 6 slices of cheese

9. One large mouth with good, strong teeth

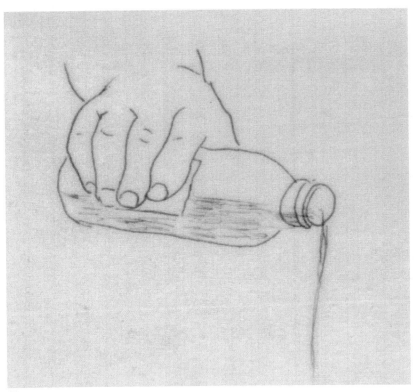

CB

THE BEST LEMON DRIZZLE

Sarah Bailey-Williams

- 225g Butter (softened)
- 225g Castor Sugar
- 275g Self Raising flour
- 2tsp Baking powder
- 4 Eggs
- 4tbsp Milk
- 3 Lemons
- 175g Granulated Sugar
- Juice of the 3 Lemons

1. Grease and line a 30x23x4 cm tin
2. Pre heat oven 160/Gas 2
3. Bung all cake ingredients into a bowl and beat with a wooden spoon or better still into a mixer and let it do its thing till all beautifully combined!
4. Place mixture into prepared tin and bake in the middle of the oven for 35-40 mins. When springy to the touch and golden brown its done! Remove from the oven and allow to stand for about 5 mins while you juice the lemons and combine with the sugar for the topping. Drizzle this over the cake once you have removed from the tin. Cut into squares once cool and enjoy with a nice pot of English tea!

A WATERLOO FOR MY WELLINGTON

From Malek Montag

Even though I do say so myself I'm a pretty good cook. Okay, Gordon Ramsey won't need alternative employment on my account but I can hold my own in the kitchen. I love cooking. I love the creativity, the bringing together of different flavours and textures and colours into one delicious meal. However, one evening's culinary experience nearly cast all that into doubt.

Once I met a gorgeous girl and believed good food and a demonstration of my culinary skills would win her heart. So, I arranged a romantic night in with her at chez author. For this mouth-watering feast, my heart's desire suggested a fish dish. Fearing the ignominy of salmonella flavoured disaster, I plumbed for a sumptuous Beef Wellington.

Keep it simple was my motto for the date. The way I planned it was the Beef Wellington would be accompanied by mashed potato, boiled broccoli and carrot mixed vegetables and covered in a mushroom duxelles. Easy! What could possibly go wrong?

The big day came. My dream girl sat in my living room supplied with red wine. My date had arrived at half past seven and I informed her dinner would be served at eight. Everything was steaming steadily towards its destination. Even the duxelles was ready. The Wellington sat on the middle shelf of my oven cooking slowly. Very slowly. I had estimated twenty-minutes per pound in the oven then set the temperature at about 150°C lest the pastry burn. And I'd started way too late.

Eight o'clock came, and went. I checked the Wellington. The pastry cloaking the colossal joint was superb. But my Wellington, like the one Napoleon face on that June day, 1815, remained unmoved.

By nine the red wine had drained from its bottle and I was left with no choice but to send my date out for more supplies. After she'd gone I checked the Wellington. Desperation gripped me like it was preparing a live chicken for supper.

At ten o'clock reinforcements arrived in the shape of my neighbour, Mike, who only asked me for some sugar. He returned to his flat and his guests (his girlfriend and her parents) with two-thirds of my Wellington. One-third remained in my oven while another went into Mike's hastily fired-up cooker, and the third was sent spinning in his microwave.

Mike's guests were settling down to a phoned-in pizza, but seeing I was on the verge of domestic peril his girlfriend's mother rolled up her sleeves and breezed into my kitchen like Blücher bursting through a Belgian forest. We managed to rescue Wellington's supporting vegetables from becoming overcooked or cold pulp and the duxelles from resembling plaster.

When the clock ticked passed eleven my easy-peasy Beef Wellington was cooked. And so was my goose. What initially began as a romantic meal for two finished as a midnight feast for half-a-dozen. It would have been churlish not to invite Mike and his entourage to dinner after their efforts. They eagerly rejected the pizza for more substantial fare.

My dream girl was diplomatic about the affair but I had to tackle the mountain of washing up on my own. My date grabbed a cab just after midnight and left me for a sailor with a penchant for fish suppers. All that remained for me of the evening was the memory of a gorgeous pastry and a plateful of "What ifs".

You can find me on:

Twitter: @Malek_Montag15

Facebook: facebook.com/malek.montag

Jean Simpkins

Top tip from that Sarah Bailey Williams in Sussex:

There is no need to open the oxo cube packet before crushing the oxo cube. Simply pull out the folded corners and flatten its between thumb and forefinger. The foil in which the cube is wrapped is designed for precisely this!

SALMON MOUSSE

Mireille Tomono, New Caledonia

Gently poach 200 gr of salmon.

I use liquid cream with around 20% fat content; if you use a thinner cream the mousse will not hold together

- 1 onion, finely chopped
- 20 cl liquid cream
- 3 soup spoons mayonaise
- 1 sachet of Madeira jello
- 3 leaflets of edible gelatin
- 6 gherkins, chopped
- garlic to taste
- pepper and juice from 1 lemon

Mix the salmon with the onion, the fresh cream, the mayonaise, the gherkins and the garlic. Boil half a bowl of water and add the jello and gelatin, softened up in cold water. Wait for it to go cold and then mix all together, cool it and at the last minute add the lemon juice.

This is quick to do and makes a delicious snack or starter. Eat with fresh crunchy bread or toast.

You cannot make a soufflé rise twice.

Rooseveldt

SAUSAGES WITH CHICKPEAS AND SPINACH

Charmayne Polsih, Slovenia

Four one-pot dishes.

Why create extra washing-up when you can cook it all in one pot? Here are four versatile dishes that either combine protein, carbs and veg all in one pot, or just need a side of good bread to complete. All recipes serve 4.

- Sunflower oil
- 2 medium onions, finely sliced
- 4 garlic cloves, smashed and chopped
- 8 good butcher's sausages, cut into four
- 400g tin tomatoes
- 400g tin chickpeas
- Bag of baby spinach
- Salt and pepper to taste
-

Gently heat the oil and then add the sausages. Brown all over and remove. Sauté the onion for 3 or 4 minutes and then add the garlic for a further 2 minutes, stirring all the time to avoid burning.

Add the sausages, tomatoes and chickpeas. Season, cover and simmer for approx. 20 minutes. Wash the spinach if necessary and add to the stew. Allow to wilt for 2 or 3 minutes. Taste and season.

Variation: You could add a finely chopped red chilli, seeds removed, when you cook the onions.

CHICKEN WITH ROASTED PEPPERS

- Olive oil
- 4 chicken portions (preferably thigh, skin on, bone in)
- 6 red and/or yellow peppers
- Punnet of cherry tomatoes
- 4 or 5 whole garlic cloves
- Juice of a lemon
- Chopped mint
- Salt and pepper to taste
- Crusty bread to serve

Heat the oven to 180 C/345F.

Slice the peppers into three or four, discarding the seeds and white ribs. Halve the tomatoes. Put them all into a large oven proof dish with the chicken pieces and tuck the garlic cloves in among it all. Season to taste. Cook for approx. 40 minutes or until cooked through.

Pour over the lemon juice and return to the oven for 5 minutes. Remove and scatter over the chopped mint. Serve with crusty bread.

Variation: instead of serving with bread, use a bigger pot and tuck tiny potatoes in with the chicken. Black olives make a good addition.

MEDITERRANEAN COUSCOUS

- 200g couscous
- 60g sunblush tomatoes, roughly chopped
- 200g cherry tomatoes, halved
- 50g pitted black olives, roughly chopped
- 1 clove garlic, crushed
- 1 tbsp capers, rinsed
- 2 tbsp green pesto
- 6 tbsp olive oil
- 1 tub mozzarella pearls or one ball of mozzarella chopped
- Fresh basil, shredded

Put the couscous into a bowl and pour over 200ml boiling water. Cover the bowl with a tea towel and leave for 10 mins until the water is absorbed.

Mix together the tomatoes, olives, garlic, capers, pesto and half the olive oil. Stir into the couscous, fluffing it up with a fork as you go. Stir in the remaining olive oil and add the drained mozzarella. Sprinkle over the shredded basil leaves.

Variation: to make a more substantial meal, places slices of warm cooked chicken or salmon on top.

SPAGHETTI WITH SALMON

- 300g spaghetti
- 4 salmon fillets
- 300g asparagus, trimmed
- Olive oil
- 75g chopped green olives
- 75g Parmesan, shaved
- salt and pepper to taste

Bring a large pan of salted water to the boil and add the spaghetti, stirring well to stop it clumping together. Simmer for 5 mins.

Carefully place the salmon on top of the pasta, cover and cook for 5 mins, over a low heat.

Add the asparagus and cook for a further 2 minutes.

When cooked, carefully removed the asparagus and salmon. Drain the spaghetti and return it to the pan. Add the asparagus, olives, olive oil and seasoning and mix well.

Transfer to warmed bowls, top with the salmon and serve with Parmesan shavings.

Variation: try it with smoked haddock or big fat tiger prawns.

MP

Tell me what you eat and I'll tell you what you are.

Savarin

THE TASTES OF HOME

Alix Norman, Cyprus

Cyprus is the island of love. A love of food. Because here, in a country that has always prided itself on its warm, Mediterranean welcome, food equals friendship. Without food, there can be no forming of relationships, renewal of long-standing attachments or even inconsequential gatherings. 'Come for coffee' merits a four-course feast; elevenses is an exercise in gastronomic caution; and a lunch invite requires a preparatory 24-hour fast! From mid-morning pastries (melt-in-the-mouth cheese tiropitas; eliopitas that are more olive than pie) to the mouth-watering dishes of the evening mezze, this is a warm and giving culture. Built on the sharing of food.

I've lived here for nigh on 20 years. And from the very first, it has been food which instigated my island friendships. Back then, my family had a holiday home in a mountain village, and my strongest childhood memories are of a place that rang with laughter and smelt of cooking. In summer, the clanging church bells heralded the smell of the morning coffee roast from the cafeneion. In winter, the men of the village would huddle over the zivania still at the top of the road, guffaws mingling with the pungent aroma of alcohol. And every weekend, the scent of rich goat souvla filled the valley – just writing about it makes my mouth water!

I learnt so much about food and friendship in the village: my Greek came from cracking walnuts with Antonia, who also taught me how to make carob toffee. Yiannis and Maria showed us that the ancient hooks up our chimney – whose purpose we'd puzzled over for weeks

– were for smoking lounza, and laughed with us over our first, blackened efforts.

Everyone in the village was, it seemed, a gastronomic wizard. Paraskevi was known for her delectable goat's cheese; a visit to her two children meant plates of luscious, feather-light halloumi. Androniki made sujuko – I'd often lend a hand, dipping long strings of almonds into a concoction of grapes before reaping the sweet, sticky rewards. And Kyproulla, the baker, always had time for the little blonde girl who'd appear in her street at six in the morning for the day's first, fresh loaf. Never a day went by when we weren't invited for a meal with neighbours, and every hour would bring a new offering left on our street-facing windowsill: succulent grapes in September, feather light flaounas at Easter, freshly-squeezed jugs of lemon juice to see us through the long summer afternoons.

Of course the process worked both ways: we were as keen to share our friendship and our tastes as were our newfound friends. Paraskevi's children developed a liking for Vimto; Androniki often dropped in for a cup of Earl Grey on her way down the lane; and Kyproulla's daughter became a fast friend over slices of toast – she provided the bread, we introduced her to Marmite.

Twenty-something years later, I'm still in Cyprus, though now I live in a modern house on a busy street. But, on this island, time and space have made no difference to the forming of friendships...

On summer evenings, my next-door neighbour and I sit on the verandah putting the world to rights over homemade koupepia and a glass of red. The local matriarch, Kyria Loukia, leaves bottles of hand-pressed olive oil on my doorstep in thanks for help with the shopping run. And, almost every morning, I wake up to bags of zesty lemons and freshly baked kolouri on the doorstep... Aphrodite's birthplace may be known worldwide as the island of love, but for those of us who have made it our home, it's the island of food. And friends.

Alix Norman has been a writer for nearly all of her 40 (very) odd years, and is currently the Chief Features Writer for the Sunday Mail and a freelance journalist with a thriving global practice. Follow her blog on alixnorman.wordpress.com

SR

COFFEE & WALNUT CUPCAKE

Sheila Pinney

Ingredients (makes approx 20)

- 250g unsalted butter, at room temperature
- 250g caster sugar
- 4 large free range eggs
- 250g self-raising flour
- pinch of salt
- 4 tbsp whole milk
- 2 tbsp instant coffee, mixed with 2 tbsp boiling water
- 60g chopped walnuts, plus 20 complete walnut halves
- Buttercream:
- 250g unsalted butter, at room temperature
- 550g icing sugar
- 4 tsp instant coffee, mixed with 2 tsp hot water

Preheat oven to 160 degrees (fan) or 170 (convection), and fill two muffin trays with 20 cupcake cases.

1. Whisk butter on high speed until pale
2. Switch to slow speed and add caster sugar, once it's all in, turn mixer onto high speed and cream butter and sugar until pale and fluffy
3. Meanwhile, sieve the flour and salt together, and lightly beat eggs with a fork
4. Add flour, salt, eggs, milk and coffee to the butter and sugar mixture and mix on medium speed until combined (be careful not to overmix - keep your eye on it and switch mixer off as soon as the mixture is fully combined)
5. Using an ice cream scoop, divide the cake batter between approx 20 cake cases

6. Bake for 18 mins, swap tins around, and bake for 4-8 mins more until all are light golden brown and a cocktail stick comes out clean
7. Leave in tins for 3-4 mins, then remove and place on wire racks to cool
8. To make the buttercream, whisk butter on high speed until pale
9. Switch to slow speed and slowly add remaining ingredients.
10. Once starting to look combined, cover bowl and whisk on high speed for 4-6 minutes, scraping down the sides of the bowl at intervals if necessary
11. Pipe buttercream onto cooled cupcakes, and top each with a walnut half

Tip - to avoid cake cases peeling away from the cakes, store cupcakes in cardboard cake boxes rather than tupperware or cake tins

Copyright Mrs Pinney's Pantry, 2015

JAFFA CUPCAKES

Mrs Pinney's Pantry

Makes 9-10

Cupcake Ingredients

- 125g unsalted butter or baking spread (at room temperature)
- 125g caster sugar
- 125 self-raising flour
- Pinch of salt
- 2 large free range eggs (at room temperature)
- 2 tbsp whole milk
- 150g orange curd
- Orange flowerpaste decorations or mini Jaffa Cakes to decorate (optional)

Buttercream Ingredients

125g unsalted butter (at room temperature)
175 icing sugar
100g dark chocolate
Dash of whole milk

Method:

- Preheat oven to 160 degrees C (fan) and line a muffin tin with 9-10 cupcake or muffin cases
- Soften butter in mixer
- Add caster sugar and mix on high until pale and fluffy

- Meanwhile sieve flour and salt together, and lightly beat eggs with a fork
- Add flour, salt, eggs and milk to the sugar and butter mixture
- Mix on slow speed until just combined
- Scoop into 9-10 cupcake cases
- Add 1 heaped tsp of orange curd to the centre of each filled cupcake case, then use the spoon handle to gently swirl the curd into the batter
- Bake for 18-25 mins until golden brown (turning after 15 mins if your oven bakes unevenly like mine!)
- Leave cupcakes in tins for 3-5 mins, then remove from tins and place on a wire rack to cool completely
- Make the buttercream by mixing the butter on high speed until pale and fluffy
- Slowly add the icing sugar, then cover and switch to high speed for 4-5 mins
- Meanwhile, melt the chocolate gently
- Add the warm chocolate and milk to the buttercream and whisk on high until well combined and fluffy
- Pipe roses using a 2D nozzle, and decorate each cupcake with orange flower paste decorations or mini Jaffa Cakes

An interesting bio from Mrs Pinney:

I'm Mrs Pinney and I teach cupcake decorating workshops in my home in Bristol.

I started selling cupcakes in 2013. I was (and still am) a stay-at-home mum having given up a career in major crime, to raise my boys. In 2012 when my youngest was a toddler I had major surgery on my neck (I have an unusual condition called Thoracic Outlet Syndrome) and after a long recovery period I decided to cheer myself up by going on a cake decorating workshop, having never held a piping bag before, and was instantly hooked! I now knew how to make my cakes look pretty and kept going to cake decorating workshops, shows and demonstrations to learn more! I soon found my own style and way of doing things, and with plenty of encouragement from Mr Pinney (yes it's our real surname!) I took out insurance, had my kitchen inspected and completed a Food Hygiene course. Our kitchen (known here as 'my pantry'!) is my favourite place to be and it's cool, light and roomy, so working and teaching at home was the obvious choice...Mrs Pinney's Pantry was born!

I absolutely love sharing the tricks of the trade and enjoy treating attendees with endless pots of tea, homebaked biscuits and gifts such as cotton shopping bags, wooden spoons and recipes to take home, along with the cupcakes they decorate themselves. I can't believe how popular the workshops are and almost always have a waiting list!

Soon after I started the business I was approached by Bristol-based Wallace & Gromit Grand Appeal to create Gromit Unleashed cupcakes for their events, I couldn't believe it! This lead to creating themed Shaun the Sheep cupcakes for them in 2015 during the Shaun In The City trail. The Gromit and Shaun cupcakes were so popular and people on social media went crazy for them, that the charity asked me to design and run Gromit and Shaun cupcake workshops in the Gromit Unleashed Shop at Cribbs Causeway to raise funds for The Grand Appeal. These workshops were excellent fun and extremely popular! And in November the charity tasked me with helping them promote the Wallace & Gromit 'Big Bake', for which I baked a cake and cupcakes for them featuring Wallace & Gromit having a disaster with a giant bag of flour which the charity displayed at Cake International at Birmingham NEC. I am delighted and honoured to be involved with this incredible charity!

I'm constantly working on new recipes and designs and have plenty of new workshops in the pipeline for this summer, as well as developing an online shop at the moment. There's never a dull moment at Mrs Pinney's Pantry, and it's a far cry from major crime!

My website is www.mrspinneyspantry.weebly.com
Twitter: @MrsPinneys
Facebook: www.facebook.com/MrsPinneysPantry

Sally Findlay

Why the Kitchen is the Happiest Room in my House

From Martha Montour, USA.

Check out my website@
www.healthbymartha.com

What's cooking?

I confess; less than two years ago I barely used my kitchen. Oh, I kept the refrigerator and freezer stocked as well as the pantry. I heated up my frozen entrees, or put together simple meals that were basically just heated up in the microwave and just as quickly noshed down.

In fact, I have lived in homes where the kitchen was barely a small closet but managed to thrive as I didn't have any real interest in cooking or preparing much food from scratch. I often used my oven as storage for other kitchen items because it wasn't going to be needed for baking!

I justified this behaviour because I was a single person and cooking for one just seemed wasteful. Why on earth would I have wanted to spend time making a meal and then cleaning up the dishes, when I could just as simply flip a few switches and have a single plate and fork to clean?

Well, I will share with you how I came to not only use my kitchen more but to find absolute joy in doing so.

Finding the fun in food

To explain the transition from seeing my kitchen as a room to store food to my favorite place in my house I need to go back a bit.

In 2013 I felt that I was living a pretty healthy life overall and that my diet was pretty healthy too. I look back to that time now and realize that while I was making some healthy choices in my diet and in my life, there were many unhealthy choices that were keeping me from my best possible health.

For one, I ate too many prepared and packaged foods. I would try to make reasonable choices from these options of prepared foods, but ultimately how healthy can one be when the food is loaded with preservatives, GMO's, sugar, fat and sodium? It may be quick to prepare and have the "right" number grams of protein and fiber, but also too much of what we don't want for the health of our bodies.

One of the first changes I made was to cut out the packaged foods in favor of whole, fresh foods. Yes, this meant that now I would have to actually turn on the light, and flip a few other switches and maybe spend more than 5 or 10 minutes getting a meal.

At first blush, this didn't feel like a change I wanted to make. But, I knew that I was on to something so I went forward any way.

As I began taking time to cut up fresh fruit and vegetables and make a fresh salad, or stir fry something I began to feel better physically. I also started experiencing increased energy, improved digestion and clearer skin.

One success breeds another, so I kept practicing and trying out new dishes that were vegetarian and even occasionally vegan.

Now the fun could really begin! Here I was, never what would be called a "great cook" but fixing meals from scratch and finding that with a modicum of effort I was turning out some really good meals

Getting "Jiggy" with it

Over time I managed to come up with about three or four recipes that were my "go to's" for healthy meals. I discovered a lovely Eggplant lasagna and a Crock Pot recipe for Quinoa and vegetables.

Now I have a confession to make. I don't like Quinoa. There I said it. I know as a Health Coach and Vegetarian to admit not liking Quinoa is akin to admitting I'm secretly a Republican and dye my pubic hair!

I tried making it every which way and try as I might I just can't get past the texture. But, the good news is there are so many other wonderful foods that I've discovered that also pack a huge nutritional wallop!

Brown rice and wild rice both now feature in my meals with stir fried vegetables and on occasion I'll make a Thai stir fried rice that will make your mouth water!

I don't use much in the way of grain these days however. But, I've discovered Chia seeds and ground flax. Maple syrup and honey as natural sweeteners.

When I shop my cart is about 90% fresh vegetables and fruit. I no longer eat meat and dare I admit it but I'm not much for working with Tofu, and it's cousins of meat substitutes. I have had some might yummy Tofu and other meat substitutes prepared in restaurants that were exquisite. Somehow, the versions I prepare just end up tasting like "fake" meat and so I find other sources for protein.

Much like tofu, I find the pseudo cheeses to be lacking. I think for me it's more of a texture thing. But, I do one day want to live completely Vegan so I will keep an open mind as I learn to live without cheese.

In making the kitchen your happiest home, it's less about the food you choose and more about the attitude toward the food.

Let's get cooking!

I recall a time about 6 months into my kitchen attitude flip when I was setting up the makings for my dinner that night and talking to my dear Mom on the phone.

Suddenly I just felt this wave of absolute comfort and joy about being in the kitchen and making dinner. I shared with my Mom. I said "You know Mom, I think the happiest moments in my life these days are those preparing food in the kitchen". She was so delighted to hear this. After all, my Mom was the original kitchen genius! Mostly though I think she was just happy to hear that I had found a way to find happiness, and it just happened to be in the kitchen!

My dear Mom has since passed on, but now when I prepare my meal for the evening I remember that conversation and smile. I truly feel my happiest when I'm whipping up something to eat. I now do my own Juicing on a daily basis and what used to feel like this huge chore and lengthy job, now is simple and fulfilling. I use my Nutra-bullet daily and I prepare fresh fruits and vegetables on a regular basis. There are days that I spend maybe 5 hours in the kitchen and don't even notice the time. Now, there was a time that I might have spent 5 hours in my kitchen over the course of a week! Who knew that something so basic could fill my heart with so much joy?

I believe a lot of the joy comes from doing something positive for myself. Like many people in a helping industry, I often tend to put my needs last. So, when I get busy in the kitchen I am saying to myself "You are worth the time this foods takes to prepare and the nutrition it will provide". That act of self love is an important one. By golly, I'm worth whole fresh foods! I am worth so much more than a sodium laden, sugar loaded microwaved entrée`!

Make your kitchen happier

I realize not all people are vegetarians and still eat well. And many people are simply too busy with jobs and families to feel they have the time to invest in their kitchen.

But, if like me you are wishing to maybe find a bit more joy in the time spent in the kitchen there are some ideas I can share to help you along.

Find a few recipes that seem easy enough to tackle and really get you excited about making them. When shopping for the items, imagine the flavours you will taste and how good the food will be for you. You can start the dining experience when you make your list!

You might need to inventory your kitchen and fill in any voids that might keep you from enjoying your kitchen time as thoroughly. For instance, a good cutting board, a decent knife or two, recipes that you can read easily (or reading glasses kept handy as in my kitchen) and some basic staples you can keep on hand.

For me that would be things like almond milk, salt, pepper, seasonings, chia seeds, flax seed and natural sweeteners. I try to always have some fruits and vegetables in the house that are fresh. If you live where there isn't ample or ready access to fresh produce, frozen can be a second best choice. I like to keep a bag of frozen peas, some frozen edamame and more in the freezer. In the pantry I always have a few cans of beans and tomatoes.

You don't need to be fancy either. You can put together a few basic items and make some great meals. And, don't be afraid to make an entire meal even if it is only for yourself. I am fond of the saying "Cook once, eat twice". In my case it would be eat three or four times. I will make up a big batch of Moroccan Lentil stew (for instance) and have a bowl for dinner, and left over another meal or two. Meanwhile I have frozen half of it and there is another 2-3 meals when I take it to thaw.

We aren't all born to be Julia Child or Rachel Ray, but that is just fine. Just roll up your sleeves and get busy and soon you will be well on your way to experiencing your kitchen as a happy place too!

"A woman should never be seeing eating or drinking unless it is lobster and champagne."

- Lord Byron.

PASTITSIO

Anne Brewer, Oxfordshire

Meat sauce

1lb minced beef or lamb, 4 rashers streaky bacon or any bacon or I have used the Christmas leftover gammon, 1 large onion, 2 large cloves of garlic, 2 tablespoons olive oil, dessert spoon each of rosemary and thyme, marjoram, fresh if you can, a bit less of cinnamon, half a pint of good stock, 4 tablespoons tomato purée, generous pinch of sugar, salt and freshly ground pepper.

Macaroni

6oz macaroni, 2oz butter, one and half ounces plain flour, three quarters of pint of milk, 1quarter pint or a bit more of Greek yoghurt, quarter pound of cheddar, salt, pepper, nutmeg, three to four tablespoons dry breadcrumbs.

Fry the chopped onion in the hot oil until beginning to brown. Add minced meat and matchsticks of bacon and colour. Stir in the crushed garlic, herbs, spices, seasoning, tomato purée and stock. Simmer uncovered, stirring occasionally, for about 40 minutes.

Meanwhile, boil the macaroni and make a white sauce with the butter, flour and milk. Away from the heat, stir in half the grated cheese, salt, pepper, nutmeg, then yoghurt and finally the drained macaroni. (I use usually boil the macaroni first then leave to drain, then use the saucepan for the sauce, then add the macaroni back in, to save washing up,). Put half the mixture in the bottom of a casserole dish, cover with the meat mixture, then top with the remaining macaroni mixture. Sprinkle the top with the breadcrumbs and the rest of the cheese and bake uncovered at 180 for about 45 minutes.

SR

But if you're gonna dine with them cannibals
Sooner or later, darling, you're gonna get eaten . . ."
— Nick Cave

DELICIOUS VEGETARIAN DISH

Louise Elson

Serves 2

Ingredients

- 1 small onion, diced
- 1/2 red pepper, diced
- 4 cherry tomatoes, quartered
- 2 handfuls of Fresh spinach, rinsed & drained
- 2 tsp tinned sweetcorn (prefer to use fresh when we have time!)
- 1 tsp garlic, minced (can use Dry Garlic Powder as an alternative)
- 2 tbsp Green Pesto
- 3 tbsp Creme Fraiche
- 6 balls of dry Tagliatelle
- Parmesan, grated to Serve
- Black Pepper and Salt to season

Method

1. Add the onions & red pepper to a pan of oil and cook on a Medium heat for about 2 minutes, until softened. Then add the minced Garlic.

2. Add the cherry tomatos, sweetcorn & spinach to the pan and continue to cook until the spinach has started to wilt.

3. Meanwhile put the Tagliatelle pasta in a pan of boiling water and cook on a high heat until tender (takes about 5 minutes)

4. Once the vegetables have all softened, add the Pesto (we bought a jar from Leclerc but do like to make our own when we have time, recipe to come!). Stir in until the vegetables are all evenly coated.

5. Then add in the Creme Fraiche and, on a low heat, stir into the mixture until everything is coated and you have a creamy consistency. You can adjust the amount of Creme Fraiche, depending on how strongly you want the Pesto flavour to come through. Obviously less Creme Fraiche means a stronger taste of Pesto,

6. Once the Tagliatelle is cooked, drain and add into the pan with the pesto mix. Again, stir until completely coated.

7. Add Grated Parmesan and enjoy!

More of Louise's wonderful recipes are on:

louisesvegetariankitchen.webs.com

CM

BEEF CARBONNADE

Sally Carayon, France

Serves at least 6

Ingredients

- 1 kg (about 2 lbs) braising steak (remove any large chunks of fat)
- 2 tablespoons olive oil
- 2 leeks sliced
- 1 stick of celery sliced
- 5 or 6 carrots peeled and sliced
- 2 medium onions peeled, sliced and chopped
- 2 medium turnips peeled and cubed
- 1 tablespoon olive oil
- 1 heaped tablespoon flour
- 25 cl (1/4 pint) strong beer
- 25 cl (1/4 pint) stock
- 1 bouquet garni with 3 or 4 extra bay leaves

Method

- Preheat the oven to 150°C (300°F) (Gas mark 2)
- Heat 2 tablespoons of olive oil in a large frying pan and brown the meat over a high heat turning quickly then put it in a casserole dish with lid (cast iron if you have one)
- In the same large frying pan, heat 1 tablespoon of olive oil and add all of the sliced and chopped vegetables. Cover the pan and cook for about 5 minutes or so over a low heat until softened.
- Sprinkle 1 heaped tablespoon of flour over the vegetables, mix well and cook for a few minutes until absorbed.

- Add 25 cl (1/4 pint) beer and 25 cl (1/4 pint) of stock, heat until bubbling hot and pour into casserole dish.
- Add bouquet garni, cover and cook in oven for 2 1/2 hours
- Serve with potatoes, rice or boulghour wheat.

You can substitute or add any other root vegetables (parsnips, swede) or a left- over broccoli stalk chopped into small pieces (remove any hard edges)

SPICY PORK IN ORANGE SAUCE

Sally Carayon

Serves 6

Quick weekday dish - can be made on one hob ring where necessary!

- 800gr - 1kg (approx 2.2lbs) pork (i used a roast fillet of pork about 6euros)
- 2 onions chopped
- 1 tin of mushroom pieces drained or fresh mushrooms chopped
- A few peeled and chopped carrots (or some mixed frozen vegetables defrosted and cooked a bit in their iced water in a saucepan)
- 2 tablespoons of zaatar (i found it at an oriental supermarket here)
- 2 teaspoons of five-spice
- 1 teaspoon of cinnamon
- 1 teaspoon ground cumin
- 1dessertspoon sugar (optional)
- The juice of 5 oranges or about 1 1/2 cups of orange juice
- The juice of 1 large lemon
- Olive oil

The night before or at least 2 hours before, cut the pork into cubes and marinate it in the fridge in the fivespice, zaatar, cinnamon and cumin and enough olive oil to coat the pork plus a bit.

Brown the meat in its oil/spice mixture in a pan, set the meat aside. Brown the onions in the rest of the oil/ spice mixture, add the mushrooms, carrots or mixed vegetables, then add the sugar.

Pour in the orange juice and lemon juice. Heat until bubbling, add the meat, cover the pan with a lid and cook on the very lowest heat for 35 minutes.

Serve with rice or couscous or bulghour wheat (I used bulghour wheat, takes about 7mins).

Phillip Davies

"Everything you see I owe to spaghetti."
— Sophia Loren

CM

Did you know .... ? Bon appetit is pronounced *bon appeteeee.*

TALENT SCHOOL TEA

Gilly P-T, Staffordshire Moorlands, England

This was made in a great rush for my daughter every Thursday afternoon in the time it took to get in from school, shortly after half past three, and get out again at about four to catch the coach to get to Talent School,(for promising young musicians)....change out of school uniform into civilian clothing, discuss the school day, and make sure daughter had music, violin, notes, pencil case, flute, homework, drink..... The meal had to be very quick to make, not too chewy to eat, and be suitably nourishing:

- Boil a pan of water, throw in enough pasta for hungry daughter, and whilst it's doing, chop some broccoli into florets, not too small.

- When it's half way cooked throw the broccoli into the pan with pasta until just done but not overdone.

- Drain it and put back in the pan with a spoon of pesto (shop bought), and a spoon of Greek yoghourt, cream or both even. Put onto a plate.

- Grate cheese over, and perhaps throw on some black olives for extra flavour. (A rasher of bacon could be fried as well and chopped and mixed in to the pasta, as a variation.)

-

Daughter should by that time be ready to sit and eat!

CB

Did you know?

On an American menu the main dish is usually called the "entrée".
An "Entrée" is in fact a starter and it means "entrance", ie entrance
to the meal. Confusing !

In Italian, the starter is the anti-pasti, meaning "before the pasta".

The French say "entrée" of course. On a menu in Spain it is usually
the "entrada".

HUNGARIAN BELL PEPPERS

From Gyuri Guti, Hungary.

During a long journey I stayed 2 months volunteering in a backpackers hostel on the shore of the Caribbean Sea in Belize. We were having discussions with some of the guests about the typical dishes of our nationalities. This is how I got the idea to prepare a delicious Hungarian dish called tojásos lecsó - bell pepper and tomatoes cooked on onions for a long time and mixed with eggs at the end. When I went to the market to get the ingredients I had to realize that there's no similar kind of pepper to that is used for this meal in Hungary. Since I really like to experiment with new things I sad to myself - I'm gonna improvise. I bought bell peppers - the big, fat and juicy ones. I couldn't wait to get home and start cooking smile emoticon the day before I already announced my plan to my friends from the hostel so they were also looking forward to taste this meal.

Here's how it goes: chop onions and put it in hot oil (lard, butter or coconut oil is also good) until it starts to get brown. Than add the chopped bell peppers and tomatoes. Do not add extra water since the veggies contain a lot. Add salt and pepper and cook until the most of the water from the vegetables disapper - depending your taste you can prepare it rather juicy or almost dry as well. Stir it regularly. It's almost done! When the veggies are soft enough and there's not much water left add eggs - mixed in a separate pot beforehand. Stir continuously and cook until the eggs are well cooked.

Ready to serve!

There were quite a few of my friends at the table, a couple from Finland, a Danish girl, a Guatemalan boy and a Belizian girl. We all liked it, I was glad to be able to share something from my culture with these people from different countries.

Even though I didn't know at the beginning how it's gonna turn out I was overly satisfied with the result. Far away from Hungary, sitting on the shore of the Caribbean Sea having lunch with folks of four different nationalities, with the taste of a traditional Hungarian meal in my mouth for a moment I felt like being at home.

Frances Black

GUILT FREE CAESAR DRESSING

I came across this when I was researching vegan recipes and I've given it a few tweaks. Now most people who know me will tell you I'm not easily impressed with fads or trends, but this is different, it works AND it's really delicious. A guilt free Caesar salad, yes, that's what I'm giving you right here. The silken tofu is the substitute for the egg and oil emulsion (& the calories). You can find silken tofu in a good health food shop. The textural crunch that is so essential in Caesar salad is not going to come from oil drenched croutons, but from cooked, grated Parmesan.

Ingredients

- 350g package of silken tofu
- 30g freshly grated Parmesan cheese
- 2 large cloves of garlic, peeled and crushed
- Juice of 1 lemon
- 1 tsp Dijon mustard
- A good splash of Worcestershire sauce
- Salt and pepper

Method

- Chuck it all in a liquidiser or use a stick blender. Puree all the ingredients together, taste and check for seasoning. Store in a lidded container in the fridge, should last about a week.
- Parmesan Crumbs
- Pre heat your oven to 180c/350f/Gas 6
- Method
- Put spoonfuls of freshly grated Parmesan cheese onto a baking sheet, lined with parchment paper. Put in the oven for about 5-8 minutes until the cheese has melted. Don't let it get too

brown or it will taste bitter. It will crisp up as it cools. When it is completely cold, crumble it over your freshly dressed leaves.

- Sometimes I like to char-grill the lettuce, it brings out the sweetness.

LEEK TERRINE

Serves 6

You will need:
2 plastic containers measuring 15x16x5.5cm

For the leeks
- 12 leeks, trimmed to 15cm lengths
- 3 litres water
- 3 tsp sea salt

For the vinaigrette
4 Tbsp. Hazelnut oil
1 Tbsp. Champagne vinegar
Pinch of sea salt
Pinch of freshly ground black pepper
Garnish
A small handful of toasted, chopped hazelnuts and some finely snipped chives.

Method

1. Mix all the ingredients for the vinaigrette by whisking in a small bowl.
2. Line one of the containers with a double sheet of cling film, making sure there is an overhang.
3. In a large pot, bring salted water to a rolling boil and cook leeks until tender, 10 minutes approximately.
4. Drain and leave to cool.
5. Layer the leeks tightly in the lined container brushing with a little bit of the vinaigrette; continue layering until container is full.

6. Fold over the overhanging cling film and place the second plastic container on top and fill it with 1kg of weight (you could use tins of beans). Store overnight in the fridge.

To serve, lift terrine gently out of its container keeping the cling film in place. Using a very sharp knife slice into even portions and using a palette knife, transfer a slice to the centre of each plate, remove cling film.

Nap with some vinaigrette, a sprinkling of chopped hazelnuts and snipped chives

FLOWER OR BERRY ICE BOWL

An extremely pretty way of serving desserts

Equipment needed

- 2 bowls, one slightly smaller than the other.
- Gaffer or masking tape
- Flowers and/or berries, leaves etc.

Make sure you have enough space in your freezer for this.

Boil a kettle full of fresh water three times, allowing it to get completely cold after each boil. This gets rid of any impurities and makes the ice bowl crystal clear. Put the smaller bowl inside the larger bowl and tape the top edges together, making sure the space is even all around. Pour in some of the water and start to gently push the flowers or berries down into the base of the bowl. Place in the freezer for an hour. Remove from the freezer and repeat with another layer of your flowers or berries and pop back into the freezer. Repeat until the outer bowl is full to the brim, store in the freezer. When you want to use it, dip the base of the larger bowl, briefly, into some warm water. Rest the ice bowl on a nice white napkin and don't leave a spoon in it, it would melt the edge of the bowl. Your imagination is the only thing holding you back here, use herbs, slices of lemon, leaves, baby vegetables or whatever you feel is appropriate for what you are serving in the ice bowl. Wipe it with a clean wet cloth when you're finished and store in the freezer, in the original bowls.

A regular contributor to Image Interiors & Living magazine, Lesley is a graduate from the prodigious Ballymaloe Cookery School and has had an impressive career in the food industry and loves nothing more than an afternoon working in her allotment.

Lesley Tumulty,
Image Interiors Magazine
lesley.ie

CB

"My weakness has always been food and men."

Dolly Parton

QUICK-QUICK CHICKEN

Manie Larsson, Holland

This dish is great for the calorie-conscious.

Quantities can vary according to taste and to how many of you are eating.

Chop some chicken breast up and place in a couple of cms of water. Poach gently till cooked. Squeeze the juice of one lemon on top of the chicken, while it is still poaching.

Chop up sweet pepper (quite small) and spring onions (normal onions will do, or leeks) and poach these in the same lemony water. You may need to add more of both lemon and water as you go. Add seasoning and any herbs you wish.

Drain thoroughly and place back in the pan with a very small amount of oil. It is best to baste the ingredients, using a little brush, so as not to use more oil than necessary. Cook slowly and add plenty of chopped mushrooms and garlic.

If you are not worried about calories, serve with mayonnaise or mix some cream in. If you are concerned about calories, this dish is delicious with mustard and slices of cold tomato.

Work is the curse of the drinking classes. Oscar Wilde.

BREAKFAST GRANOLA

Vivien Houghton, England.

Ingredients	Original recipe	Alternative
Jumbo oats	450g	500g
Sunflower seeds	120g	250g
Pumpkin seeds	none	none
Sesame seeds	120g	
Almond crumbles	250	
Hazelnut crumbles	none	400g min
Walnut crumbles	none	
Pine nuts	none	few
Ground ginger	tsp	1.5 tsp
Ground cinnamon	2 tsp	2.5 tsp
Maldon salt	1 tsp	1 tsp
Apple sauce	175g	
Syrup	120g	0-100g to taste
Honey	4 tbl sp	200g
Light brown sugar	100g	none
Sunflower oil	2 tbl sp	none
Walnut/hazelnut oil	none	2 tble sp

Raisins	300g	
Sultanas	none	300g
Cranberries	none	

Method

- Mix everything together well except raisins, sultans, cranberries

- Spread onto oven tray.

- Bake at 170 degrees for up to an hour

- Bake at 140 degrees

- Turn regularly until evenly brown

- Turn every 20 mins till done

- When cool add raisins etc

CB

YUMMY SOUP

Pippa Taylor, Sussex

Ingredients

- 1/2 butternut squash
- 1/2 celeriac
- 1 sweet potato
- 4 shallots
- 4 garlic cloves
- 4 smallish potatoes

Method

Peel and chop into medium chunks all the veg, put in roasting pan and drizzle with olive oil, black pepper and mixed herbs. Bake in oven at 180 degrees (fan) for an hour and 15 minutes. Leave to cool. Make up 1.25 litres of vegetable stock. Put in blender and mix till smooth, adding a bit of stock at a time as needed. Reheat if necessary in a saucepan and serve with warm crusty loaf slices smothered in butter.

"At a dinner party one should eat wisely but not too well,
and talk well but not too wisely."

- Somerset Maugham

BT

"Life's not fair, is it? Some of us drink champagne in the fast lane, and some of us eat our sandwiches by the loose chippings on the A597.

- Victoria Wood

CEASAR SALAD

Bob Ranyard

Serves 2

Ingredients

- 1 gem lettuce, washed and pulled apart into smaller pieces.
- 1/2 a radiccio lettuce washed and finely chopped.
- A small fistful of chives, finely chopped.
- 110gms of cooked french beans, chopped into 1 inch pieces.
- 1/2 cup of fresh toasted croutons.[about four slices of french stick will do]
- Two good servings of freshly shaved parmesan cheese.
- 3 to 4 fillets of salted preserved anchovies, cut into strips.

Method

- Take a serving dish, glass or ceramic, and place your washed and prepped lettuce.
- Sprinkle the cooked and cut french beans over the lettuce.
- Then arrange the cut anchovies over the lettuce and beans.
- Then shave the parmesan or roughly grate and sprinkle over the salad.
- Finally chop the slices of french stick into 1/4s and fry in a pan in a little butter and oil.
- when golden brown sprinkle over the salad, and serve.

For the salad you will need to serve Ceaser Salad Dressing. You will need a two pint jug to make this.

- 3x dessert spoons of olive oil
- juice of two lemons
- 1 teaspoon of Worcestershire sauce
- 2x dessert spoon of creme fresh [or plain yogurt]

- 1 teaspoon of Dijon mustard
- 2x teaspoon of finely grated parmesan cheese

Whisk all together well in your jug, it will emulsify quite easily, however you can add a large spoon of mayonaise to this to help it hold together.

Pour the dressing over your salad, enjoy.

These recipes where invented by the Chef Ceaser Cardini, in 1924.

Bob Ranyard lives and works in Uckfield, East Sussex. He has collected many recipes on his frequent travels. You can connect to Bob on his website.

farrandale.simplesite.com

CM

FOR AN UPSET TUMMY

One and a half teaspoons of cumin seed. Put in strainer and pour one cup of boiling water over it in such a way that the seed sits a while in the boiling water, then leave to steep for five minutes. Sweeten with honey if required.

CB

"I never touch sugar, cheese, bread...
I only like what I'm allowed to like. I'm beyond temptation. There is no
weakness. When I see tons of food in the studio, for us and for everybody, for me it's as if this stuff was made out of plastic. The idea
doesn't even enter my mind that a human being could put that into
their mouth. I'm like the animals in the forest. They don't touch what
they cannot eat."

— Karl Lagerfeld

SOUFFLÉ AU GRAND MARNIER

Guilaine Vautrain, France

Ingredients

- 16 cl of milk
- 30 gr cornflour
- 120 gr sugar
- 40 gr butter
- 6 soup spoons of Grand Marnier
- 4 eggs + 2 egg whites
- 2 pinches of salt

Light the over at 180 ° (gas mark 6). Butter a soufflé mould and powder it with a little sugar. Separate the yolk from the white of the 4 eggs. Put the 4 whites in a bowl and add the other two. In a saucepan put three soup spoons of sugar , the cornflour and the cold milk. Beat it all thoroughly. Put the saucepan over low heat, keep stirring till it starts to boil. It will go thick quite suddenly, so avoid lumps. Remove from heat immediately but keep stirring while you add the Grand Marnier, the egg yolks and the butter. Keep stirring!

Add the 2 pinches of salt to the egg whites and beat till firm, then add the rest of the sugar. Now add a big spoonful of this to the mixture in the saucepan. Stir thoroughly and then pour the mixture over the remaining egg whites – in one hit. Stir slowly now, making sure you get it up from the bottom – use a spatula.

Now the whole lot goes in to the mould. Cook for 30 minutes and eat immediately.

Délicieux!

CM

"Tomatoes and oregano make it Italian; wine and tarragon make it French. Sour cream Russian, lemon and cinnamon Greek. Soy sauce makes it Chinese. Garlic makes it good."

- Alice May Brock

"There's a friendly tie of some sort between music and eating."
- Thomas Hardy

CB

POMMES DE TERRE MONT ST.MICHEL

Also from Guilaine Vautrain in France

Peel and wash potatoes. You need ones that will not fall apart while cooking. Slice in to rounds and cook very gently in a pan of milk.

This takes about half an hour.

During this time wash 6 or 7 leeks and chop them up very finely. Put them in a pan to cook along with a little salt and pepper. Watch them carefully because they must not go brown.

Drain the milk from the potatoes and then put them in a buttered over-proof dish.

Add the leeks, fresh cream and a little nutmeg. Put in a hot oven for a short while to warm through thoroughly.

Delicious with lamb chops.

CB

Top tip: When feeding a fussy child, cut out the middle-man. Just cook the food and put it in the bin.

SR

"If more of us valued food, and cheer, and song above hoarded gold, it would be a merrier world. "

- Tolkien.

HUMBLE PIE

Rania MM Watts, Palestine

cementcoveredinkquills.blogspot.ca

We are not perfect beings throughout our lives; I believe it is necessary to consume a massive slice of humble pie every-now-and-again to balance our: pride and dignity.

I sought a secret family recipe from the days of old. Unfortunately, my provisions have been completely depleted.

An essential ingredient for the dough must be harvested; the bark from an extremely aged and wise willow.

I do comprehend that trees are ubiquitous!

I found the perfect tree right across the one I used last time. This trunk occupies a width of one to two meters in length.

It is integral that I be careful with my scalpel and scrapper; as I do not want to damage this exquisite chimera. I remembered from last time, the four inch square pieces were to large for me to grind; which is why I had to alter the recipe for one inch squares instead.

Now, that I have collected 2 baskets worth I am required to ground, to a fine flour texture with an ancient pestle and mortar. All thatI need now is about ½ cup of tree sap: blend and roll out the crust.

Once my crust is ready all I require to complete this recipe - patiently waits for me in my pantry:

3 phoenix eggs for balance 2 ground lavender sprigs for endurance 1 tablespoon of juice from the bitterest lemon1 cup of freshly ground sugar cane for sweetness of desire ¾ cup tear drops from a horrible failure for remembrance ¾ cup fresh giggles for eternal happiness1 rotten ostrich egg for the coyote ugly factor Hand blend all of my ingredients well, this will ensure that the filling is riddledwith human comfort and expression.

Place in oven at sunrise and take out mid-morning. Humble pie is severed best warm with a slice of Swiss cheese or Vanilla ice cream.

Voila! Bon Appetit!!!

CB

Did you know ... ? there is a difference between Caribbean "rice and beans" and "beans and rice". Rice and beans is rice with a bean dish on top, whereas with beans and rice the two are mixed together.

MUCKY MANGO CHUTNEY

Amanda Wren-Grimwood

chezlerevefrancais.com

Sweet, spicy, sticky and tangy...who can resist this delicious home-made lime and mango chutney? I started making this by accident as I couldn't buy mango chutney here in France and now, I have to say, I prefer this. The lime pickle in restaurants in the UK is too strong for me and the mango chutney is too weak. This lime and mango chutney recipe is really easy, makes a great Christmas present and, most importantly tastes fantastic smeared on a poppadum! I bung a poppadum in the microwave for 40-50 seconds for a low calorie snack. I can't get poppadums here at all so I get everything delivered from Spices of India: Spices of India. They are brilliant and I can get all my spices in bulk within a few days, along with coconut powder which is cheaper than buying coconut milk.

This mango chutney is really easy. The hardest bit is wrestling with a mango. I hold the mango at the stalk end and slice off either side of the stone. Score it and slice off the flesh. Then hack at the stone bit!

Place the mango, sliced limes, chillies and vinegar in a pan and simmer for 15 minutes. Add sugar and salt and simmer for 40-50 minutes until the mixture is thick. Pound some cardamon pods in a pestle and mortar and extra. Dry fry the cardamon seeds with cumin and coriander and then grind to a fine powder.Add the spices to the warm mango chutney mix and then pour into sterilised jars.

This makes about 6 jars which have a shelf life of 2 years.... It won't last that long! You will be using it in a chicken sandwich or in Coronation Chicken if you are not dipping poppadums in it.

CB

"Bad men live that they may eat and drink, whereas good men eat and drink that they may live."

- Socrates

SWEET LAMB CURRY

John Holland, Australia

Ingredients

- Left over roast lamb.

- 1 middle sized onion (diced)

- 1 small tin of fruit salad

- 1 tablespoon of chutney

- 1 half cup of plump raisins

- A dry curry mix such as Keens

- Orange juice

- Salt & pepper

- Plain flour

Method

Cut the roast lamb into bite sized cubes. Fry the onion lightly (use a little virgin olive oil) once the onion is sweated down a little add the meat to brown slightly. Add the curry powder to the pan and mix until the meat is browned. Then add one or table spoons of flour. Cook for a little while longer, making sure the flour is even distributed. Add the fruit salad, raisins and chutney. Mix well. Finally add 1 to 2 glasses of orange juice and allow mixture to simmer for five minutes. Season with salt and pepper to taste. Serve with rice.

John Holland is a poet with some of his work published in Poetry Without Borders (ATLApublising.com)

More about John on poetrysansfrontieres.weebly.com

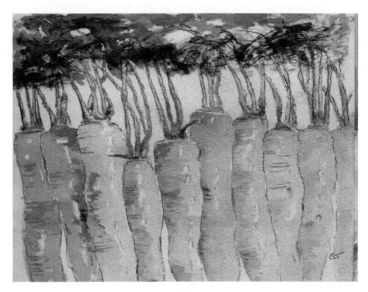

BT

"If you can eat with mates or friends or family, I mean, it's such a brilliant thing isn't it? If you feel really rubbish and you have a nice bit of
food it makes you feel good, you know?
"

— Jamie Oliver

Lynn Cook

SOUTHERN SCRAMBLE

Alison Neale, England

- 1 onion,finely chopped

- 2 slices ham , diced

- 1 tin tomatoes

- 4 or 5 eggs

Fry the onion off in a little vegetable oil. Add the ham and tomatoes and warm through. Beat the eggs, and add to the pan, stirring, to scramble everything. Cook on a little until the liquid is lessened, and the eggs are cooked.

Serve with some good crusty bread.

TUNA TOAST

Alison Neale

audeart.com

- Tin of tuna in sunflower oil

- Mayonnaise

- Cheddar cheese

- Fresh ground pepper

- French stick type bread

The quantities are not specific, as it depends how hungry you are!

Cut a big length of the French stick, and cut it in half. Toast it slightly under a grill on both sides.

Drain the tuna and mix with the mayonnaise until it is nice and creamy. Season with a couple of grinds of pepper.

Spread thickly on the cut side of each piece of the toasted bread, top with grated cheddar cheese and back under the grill until the cheese is bubbling.

Great with lime pickle !

MT

SWAHILI COCONUT PRAWNS OR FISH

Nicky Rodgers, Tanzania.

Serves four.

The East African coastal cuisine has a strong Asian influence, and lends itself to the abundance of seafood, fish, spices and coconut in the region. This is a wonderful dish for entertaining as the sauce can be made in advance, with coconut milk and prawns or fish added at the last minute.

- ¼ tsp coriander
- 1tsp whole black peppercorns
- 1/4tsp fenugreek seeds
- ¼ tsp mustard seeds
- 1 green chilli
- ¼ teaspoon turmeric
- 200g onions chopped
- 1 tbs tamarind paste or 1 tbs lemon juice
- 2 tbs vegetable oil
- ¼ tsp salt

- 5 fresh or dried curry leaves
- 2 cloves garlic- thinly sliced
- 1 tsp grated fresh ginger
- ½ tsp chilli powder
- 400 ml coconut milk

- 200g tomatoes, chopped.
- 200g bell pepper, sliced

- 500 g uncooked prawns.
- 500g thick fillets of haddock, halibut, pollock or any firm white fish cut into 4 chunks.

- Lightly roast coriander, peppercorn and fenugreek seeds for a minute and grind in coffee/spice grinder along with dried curry leaves if using.
- Heat oil and add mustard seeds until they pop and then curry leaves if using. Add onion and garlic. When browned add ginger.
- Add tomatoes and peppers and stir for a minute.
- Add with ground spices, curry leaves, paprika, chilli powder, turmeric, salt, chilli, and tamarind or lemon juice. Then add pepper and tomato.
- Simmer for 5 minutes or until softened and reduced. Sauce may be made in advance.

- 5 minutes before eating heat sauce on high flame in frying pan. When it bubbles add prawns and stir until opaque. Add coconut milk until it bubbles and serve.
- OR gently add fish chunks for a couple of minutes, then add stirred coconut milk and simmer gently for 5- 10 minutes until fish is cooked. Serve with plain rice.

"Only the pure in heart can make good soup."

- Beethoven.

POLENTA AND ALMOND CAKE

Clare Brown, Watford, England

Gluten free if you use gluten free baking powder.

Ingredients

- 225g butter 225g sugar
- I use half spoon so I halve the amount
- 3 eggs
- Polenta (fine cornmeal) 220g
- 100g ground almonds
- 1tsp baking powder

Method

Cream butter and sugar together, beat in the 3 eggs. Mix the polenta, almond and baking powder and add to the mix. Place in to a pre-lined square baking tin, 20 cm square. Bake for 20 mins at 180c. Ready if skewer comes out clean. Cut into squares, I sometimes put icing sugar on the top.

Lovely moist and quite yellow cake.

SR

"When engaged in eating, the brain should be the servant

of the stomach."
— Agatha Christie

MARS BAR CAKE

Ann Haycock, Wakefield, West Yorkshire

Ingredients

- 170 grams butter or margarine
- 2 tablespoons of Golden Syrup
- 5 Mars bars
- 453 grams of digestive biscuits (crushed)
- 55 gms of dried fruit (optional)
- Approximately 200 grams of milk chocolate
-

Method

- Very slowly melt Mars bars, butter and golden syrup in a large pan on a very low heat.

- Mix well until all combined. Stir in crushed digestive biscuits and put in swiss roll tin. I press down with a spoon and smooth.

- Put into the fridge until set.

- Melt chocolate and spread over top. Again, put in fridge until set.

- It is easier if you cut into squares before it sets too hard. I cut into 24.

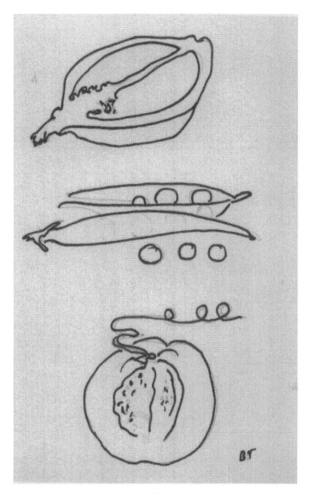

BT

Did you know?

The name of the French seafood dish <u>bouillabaisse</u> comes from the words bouillir, to boil, and baisser, to lower. Bouillabaisse means, more or less, "boil to lower".

Top cake tip from Susan Newell, Croydon, England:

Hi, when baking a sponge cake place a baking tray on the shelf above and a dish of water in the oven, lower the temperature to 160 degrees and you will have a beautiful moist flat topped cake ready for decorating (increase the cooking time by approx. 25 per cent).

SEED CRUST SPELT LOAF

Afan Arts, Wales

Ingredients

- 250g wholemeal spelt flour
- 250g strong white flour
- 2tsp easy dried yeast
- 1-2tsp fine salt
- 175ml orange juice
- 175ml water
- Pumpkin seeds
- Sunflower seeds
- Sunflower oil for brushing

Method

Grease a loaf tin with a little of the sunflower oil. Dust with spelt flour and sprinkle some of both types of seeds in the bottom, barely covering it.

Sift all the flour into a mixing bowl. Add the yeast, stir in, then add the salt. Mix the juice and water together and warm slightly until tepid.

Add to the flour mixture and mix thoroughly with your hands or with a spatula, forming into a loaf shape. Put into the loaf tin and spread out to fill it, levelling the top.

Sprinkle the top with more seeds, pushing them into the surface of the loaf with the spatula. Brush the top with oil and cover with cling film (the oil stops the loaf from sticking to the cling film as it rises).

Place the tin in a warm room to rise for about an hour or until it reaches the top of the tin. Preheat the oven to 225 degrees C and, removing the cling film, place the loaf on the middle shelf for 15mins.

After this time, turn the oven down to 190 degrees and bake for a further 25 mins. Turn the loaf out of the tin and check it sounds hollow when tapped on the bottom. You can return it upside down in the tin to the oven to bake further if needed.

Leave to cool on a wire rack.

BT

A HEART-WARMING STORY ABOUT A BREAD OVEN

From Lorraine Swoboda, Poland.

On the coldest day of the year, looking for something warm to do, we decided to try out our old bread oven. This was the old-style brick-dome variety, with an iron door, situated in its own little room in the back of the house. People had cooked this way for centuries. How hard could it be ? If you've ever seen an old cottage fireplace with one of these beside the chimney, it's the same thing. You have to light a fire inside it. You use faggots – bundles of twigs – and you keep feeding them in till the oven is very hot. The plan is to heat the bricks and to then rake out the ashes, and then use that residual heat to cook your bread. In the past the rich got the top half of the loaf and the poor got the bottom half with all the ash in it – hence our expression "upper crust".

We duly lit the fire, and waited. And fed it. And waited. A neighbour appeared. "That's no good," he said and loaded in the rest of the faggots.

You'd have thought we'd be backing out of the door to cool off with the resulting blaze, but these ovens are there to bake your bread, not you, and they don't give off heat at all.

I fetched a radiator and hot drinks. I also brought the oven thermometer, and put it just inside the door. It immediately went right off the scale (it only goes up to 350 °C). Bread cooks at a high temperature, around 220 °C, but we could probably have glazed pottery in there.

We amused ourselves elsewhere. I had prepared the dough in my modern oven in my modern kitchen. Eventually, thinking the temperature must have dropped enough, because mine had, and I was fed-up with waiting, I took one of my lovely well-risen rounded loaves outside on a tray and pushed it in to the now dark cavity. It immediately went black. I pulled it out again. We waited again. I whiled away the time cutting off the top of the loaf and covering it with foil.

Eventually we managed to cook three loaves successfully – well, two and a half – while we turned blue with cold.

Then I put a Guernsey bean pot in there, and a shepherd's pie. With that one burn of waste wood I could have cooked any number of casseroles and cakes. The next day it was till registering 150 ° °C. If I'd had one handy I'd have cooked a leg of lamb overnight, and it would have been perfectly ready for lunch.

So, to make full use of such an oven, you need a few faggots of wood, somewhere else to raise your dough, as many casseroles and stews as you can fit inside, a lot of hungry friends and neighbours, scarf, mittens, hot water bottle and a note to self to not tell the local pyromaniac your plans !

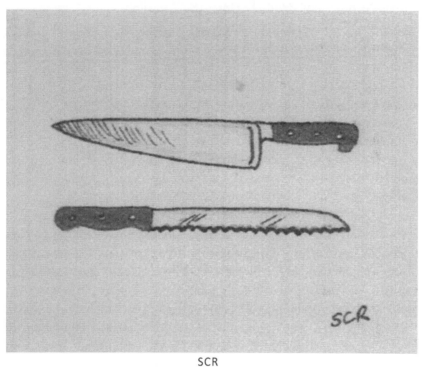

SCR

"The slogan of Hell: Eat or *be eaten. The slogan of Heaven:*
Eat and be eaten."
— W.H. Auden

THE FRENCH ÉGLADE!

Catherine Broughton gives us a humorous description of an écclade, a traditional mussel dish from the Charente Maritime part of France. This section is taken out of her book (available from Amazon) "A Call from France".

An écclade is a traditional cooking of mussels in the Charente Maritime. The entire coastline is renowned for its seafood – as indeed is any coastline, I guess – mussels and oysters being the staple diet of the local people. An entire culture has evolved around mussels and oysters, accompanied by a whole world of "knowledge" about the type of oyster or mussel, and an entire vocabulary to go with it.

For this particular speciality, the muscles are arranged, tier by tier, in a circle on a fireproof – usually a large cast iron platter - dish or even just on the sand. They are carefully balanced, facing inwards (this is important) so that they eventually make a kind of rounded pyramid. All guests must stand in a circle and admire. Pine needles are then placed over them, about two inches thick, and everybody must again admire. Words like "ooh la-la" are uttered. At a given signal (a mystery to this day) the pine needles are set alight. They are allowed to burn (along with further ooh la-la) for about three minutes and then are brushed away, hopefully onto sand or similar where they will die out. All guests then help themselves to the pine-scented cooked mussels.

This is altogether more complicated than it seems. The mussels are not only too hot to touch but also black with pine ashes, and the ones that were not facing inwards – or which fell to one side during the various ooh la-la-ings – are also filled with black pine ash. After we'd attended two or three of these functions we discovered that vast quantities of kitchen roll are essential for wiping blackened fingers, and vast quantities of chilled white wine for washing down the ash. Even so, we didn't bother with them again.

More about Catherine Broughton on www.turquoisemoon.co.uk

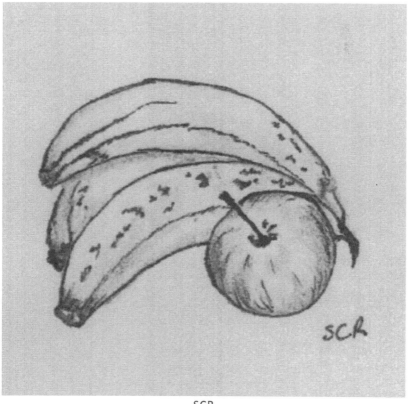

SCR

Did you know ... ? that if you crush garlic gloves a fraction under the flat of a knife, it makes them easier to peel.

TASTY VEGGIE WRAPS

From Brian Thornton,   Afan Arts.

Serves 2, takes 20 minutes.

Ingredients

- Tortilla wraps

- 1 onion (white or red)

- 1 sweet potato,

- 1 tomato

- garlic

Method

Fry the onion for 3 minutes with one or two cloves of garlic in olive oil. Chop the sweet potato into small cubes and add to the onion. Cook until soft and then add the chopped tomato.

Heat a frying pan and add a tortilla (no need for oil). Warm and turn over. Cook the other side for a minute or so until it is brown and add a line of the above filling about a third of the way up the wrap. Roll the wrap up into a thick cigar shape and serve.

You can serve with a crispy lettuce salad with avocado if you like or a red onion and tomato salad or, if you prefer a warm accompaniment you can fry a small onion (or shallot) until well browned add a tea spoon or so of brown sugar and then a tin of tomatoes. Drizzle a little red wine vinegar or some balsamic vinegar over the sauce when it is ready to serve. If you like something hotter, split a chilli and add to the onion as it is cooking for a spicy chilli tomato sauce.

Alternatives - there are so many that this really is a meal that you can make with almost anything. Try adding parsnip to the sweet potato mix, or use some quorn chicken cubes as well as the sweet potato, a little red pepper works well too.

You can use a refried bean recipe for the filling instead of the sweet potato one given here - just fry the onion with the garlic (heavy on the garlic!) until well browned and then add a tin of borlotti beans and mash the mix to then fill the wraps. This is nice if you also add some avocado and fresh tomato to the wrap. Try adding some sun dried tomato to the wrap too. A South American version is to have the refried beans with chilli and add a fried egg with a little avocado, they have this for breakfast with the spicy tomato sauce and, although it may sound odd, it does start the day with a bang and is very tasty.

SR

FOR A CHILD WHO IS UNWELL AND WON'T EAT

Andree Brown

Find one of those dishes that is split in to several parts, ie for cocktails snacks, or a small lazy susan. In each section put different things – jelly in one, yoghurt in another, raisins in a third, grated cheese ... and so on.

It doesn't matter whether or not the food "goes" together – the child doesn't mind. The different sections will interest him and he will eat a little from each part.

Alternative (or for the second meal), cut the crusts off a slice of buttered bread (because children don't like crusts and the aim here is to get him to eat – worry about not "spoiling" him another day!) Put the slice on a plate and cut out two slices of cucumber for eyes.

A blob of mayonnaise in the middle will hold a raisin in place for the centre of the eyes.

A small triangle of cheese makes a nose and a slice of tomato, cut in half, makes a smile. The hair can be grated carrot or grated cheese. Or anything similar.

CB

"My message is, as it always has been, moderation: meat as a main course on three days a week, eggs on one, fish on one other and some form of vegetarian meal on the rest constitute a perfectly acceptable, interesting and varied diet."
— Delia Smith.

NANNA'S BACON HOT POT

Shelley Dootson, Greenland

Makes: 4 for a small dinner

Ingredients

- 2kg red potatoes
- 1 pack (8 rashers) smoked trimmed bacon
- 1 large onion
- salt and white pepper

Method

1. Peel and chop potatoes into 1/2cm thick (try to keep all the potatoes roughly the same thickness for an even cooking), dice onion into fairly small pieces and cut bacon into 1cm thick bites.

2. In an ovenproof dish, layer the onion then potato, seasoning and bacon till all are used.

3. Place a lid on top and oven cook slowly for 2-3 hours till potatoes are soft.

OYSTERS

Amanda Wren-Grimwood, France

I can't believe I only discovered oysters three years ago! I always thought I was adventurous with food but I never really fancied the idea of swallowing something live and raw. When I finally plucked up the courage to try one in Loch Fyne in Portsmouth, I couldn't believe how mad I'd been to wait for so long. Unfortunately, although we used to live near the sea, we could only buy them at the docks or at Loch Fyne.

Now, I have absolutely no excuse as all the large supermarkets in France stock them all the time. The French people love them, especially as a traditional starter at Christmas. There are huge queues and often they set up a special stall in the car-park or in another part of the shop.

So the supply problem was sorted. Then there is just the teensy problem of preparing them especially when you have a lovely guy in the next hamlet who loves fishing and comes back from the coast with a vast bucket of oysters!

Here's what you do:

First get yourself a shucking knife. We have one for 99 cents. It is just a strong pointed knife which is sharp on both sides. We also have one with an extra lever so you can nip off a piece off the edge of the shell if you can't find a place to put the knife in. The oysters might need a scrub and a rinse. Otherwise, when they are opened grit can get in.

Hold your oyster with the flattest bit uppermost; you don't want to spill any of the juices when you open it.

Insert your knife and start to wiggle. You might want to wear a leather glove or hold it with a tea-towel.

Carefully move the knife all around the edge.

With a little twist it should pop open!

You can then loosen the oyster if you want.

Serve individual portions if you like. I prefer to put a layer of crushed ice on a platter and scatter lemon wedges across so everyone can help themselves. Athough I am usually given a little fork to loosen the oyster in restaurants I have to say that a grapefruit spoon is much more effective. They are often served with Tabasco and finely chopped shallots in red wine vinegar. A little bit of crusty bread and butter always goes down well too...

They are often served open in the UK but the French serve them with the shells put back so that's how we do it now. Pour yourself a nice chilled glass of Muscadet Sur Lie and enjoy!

chezlerevefrancais.com

Did you know ... that ostrich meat contains almost no fat?

SCOTCH EGGS

also from chezlerevefrancais.com

If you mentioned Scotch eggs to me a few years ago I would be transported back to 70's buffets. Tinned ham, corned beef, home-made pickled onions, which would take the lining from your mouth, and other delicacies such as piccalilli, pork pie and the un-forgiving stain of beetroot all over the plate.

The Scotch eggs would be served cold; an egg in a very non-descript sausage layer, all encased in a lurid orange sawdust crumb. Nowa-days the humble Scotch egg has been elevated to bistro level, mashed with chorizo or black pudding and served hot and oozing and nothing at all like I remember.

When I was back in the UK before Christmas I had Scotch eggs at Cams Mill and I had a real yearning to recreate them at some point. As it turned out Christmas arrived and I picked up some quail eggs thinking I would use them in various dishes. For some reason they were still there, perhaps because they were so pretty. I always have good sausage-meat on hand which is 'farcé à légumes' here but in the UK I would buy good quality sausages or used minced pork shoulder.

The secret with Scotch eggs is to get everything ready. Prepare three bowls with flour, eggs and breadcrumbs. I used fresh brown bread whizzed in the food processor. Season the sausage-meat and add the herbs. It makes it easier if you divide the sausage-meat into portions before you start. Boil the eggs for 2 minutes if you want a runny middle. I boiled for three minutes as quail eggs are fiddly to shell. Flatten the sausage-meat into a circle with floured hands.

It is definitely a bit fiddly but shape the sausage-meat around the egg. It's easier if you cup it in your hand and gently cover the egg.

AS you shape each one I find it's easier to put them in flour straight-away and then place on a board whilst the rest are shaped.

Once they have all been shaped and dipped in flour dunk them in the beaten egg and then breadcrumbs.

It's best to stick the lot in the fridge for 30 minutes or so to firm them up.

Deep fry at 180 C for four minutes and enjoy them while they're hot with red onion chutney or a bit of mustard, lovely!

Shop bought Scotch eggs? Nah....

"Eating is a genuine need, continuous from our first day to our last, amounting over time to our most significant statement of what we are made of and what we have chosen to make of our connection to home ground."

— *Barbara Kingsolver*

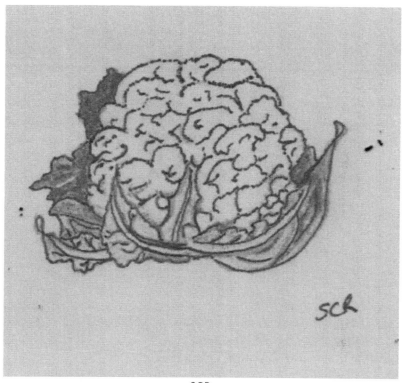

SCR

Did you know ... ? That vinaigrette (pronounced vinaigre<u>tt</u>) means simply (near as damn it) "a little vinegary thingy" !

ARTICHOKE BAKE

Jan Cooper, England/France

Serves 4

A very easy & tasty starter, serve with lots of crusty bread and dip away.

Ingredients

1 Tin artichokes – drained & roughly chopped

2-3 garlic cloves – crushed

3 tablespoons of good full fat mayonnaise

70g pack of parmesan

Method

Pre heat oven to 200C
Grease 4 ramekins
Mix all ingredients with half of the parmesan
Spoon into greased ramekins
Sprinkle over remainder of parmesan
Bake in oven for 20 to 25 minutes until golden brown

SCR

Why did the student eat his homework ?

Because the teacher told him it was a piece of cake !

TCHE-TCH-OUKA

Fatima Nazir, Algeria

Chop 2 onions. Slice 3 sweet peppers, choosing one yellow pepper, one red and one green. Fry the onions in sunflower oil – you need the oil to be around 1 cm deep – till soft, stirring regularly.

Add the peppers and 3 or 4 cloves of chopped garlic. Keep stirring. Add a tin of chopped tomatoes, 2 teaspoons of tomato puree, some herbs of your choice, a little salt and pepper.

Cook it all over a slow-medium heat. Serve with any kind of meat and potato wedges.

This dish freezes well and is a good stand-by for almost any meal.

CB

"I eat my peas with honey,
I've done it all my life.
It makes the peas taste funny,
But it keeps them on the knife ..."
- Bruce Broughton

CHESTNUT DELUXE

Lorraine Swoboda, England/France

Take one carton of plain Greek yoghurt for two people; add one small tin of sweetened chestnut purée, and stir until well-mixed. You can add a tablespoon of double cream or fromage frais depending how wicked you're feeling. You can grate dark chocolate over the top if you like, but it's good whichever way you make it.

Did you know ...? That if you take a few drops of aniseed several times a day when you are travelling in third world countries, it can protect you from upset tummies. Add to a piece of bread or similar or simply put a few drops in to your water.

SCR

SNAILS

From Catherine Broughton

turquoisemoon.co.uk

When the weather is damp (and this year we have had a lot of damp) my cleaning lady, Josie, comes round to pick up snails.

She lives in a flat, you see, and the grounds around the blocks of flats are already covered by other tenants picking up snails whereas she, being the cleaning lady for the Chateau, has large snail-gathering grounds at her disposal.

She arrives with a carrier bag. If I am feeling helpful I will sometimes go round the grounds with her and help her gather snails for her free-bee supper.

"Only the big ones please, Madame, the small ones are bitter and too much trouble," she instructed me – but in French, of course.

Dutifully I pull snails off gate posts and fences and pop them in to Josie's carrier bag. It is remarkable how many there are and how large they can be. If you are intending to make them your main meal of the day, you need a helluva lot of them.

"What do you do with them? Boil them?"

"Ah non, Madame! Non, non, non, non!!" (It's okay, Josie, I got the first non, don't repeat it). "You must never boil them. That is the worst thing you can do."

"I see," I said, wishing I hadn't asked.

"You need a cardboard box," said Josie, "and some flour."

I wondered if she had perhaps moved the conversation on to something totally different, when she continued:

"Quite a deep cardboard box," she said, "so that there's no chance of the snails getting out. You sprinkle plenty of flour in first, see, plenty of flour. Season it well, especially with pepper. Me, I put in a touch of salt, plenty of pepper and lots of garlic. As much garlic as you have got. The more the better."

"Jolly good," I said.

"The snails move about in the flour," she explained. "They get themselves all sort-of clogged-up in it. They leave this kind of slime behind them, and that mixes in with the flour. Makes a good sauce."

"Ugh! Doesn't sound too good, Josie, " I said.

"But it is, Madame, it is delicious. You leave the snails several days. If you have put lots of salt in, you can leave them longer. Then you fry them up in a spot of oil, add more garlic – and voila! Very good, they are, very good. Glass of white wine, bit of bread, and it's lovely. You should try it. In fact, Madame, if we gather a few more, I'll make some for you too!"

"Ah – no, no worries. We have already tried them actually. Wasn't our thing. Thanks all the same."

Josie gave me a sideways look.

"I've heard about how the English eat," she half-whispered. She gazed at me in awe. "You prefer to put jam on your meat, don't you? Is it true?!"

From The Very Round Café and Tea Rooms, USA

I had a neat little café at the edge of town. Business was good. Nothing super-human, but good, and we made a living. It was real hard work. We got up, my wife Hilda and me, early every morning. One of us went to the market while the other got the place ready for breakfast meals. We opened at 7.00 each morning, served an average of 20 breakfasts, all prepared and cooked by ourselves, then closed at 11.00 which gave us just enough time to clean everything and get ready for the mid-day meal customers.

We closed again, after a very busy time serving 20-30 lunches, at 3.00. This gave us time for a bite to eat, rest up, and another clean-up before dinner. We closed at 11.30 at night. We were open seven days a week, except we didn't do breakfast on Sundays.

It was hard work, but it was also fun. Sometimes we made enough to pay somebody to come in and help, sometimes two people. We went on like this for over six years.

Then one day we got a bad review saying we seemed to be always closed. Somebody replied to the review, saying that they had been in at 2.30 and had had to rush their meal because we were closing.

This was upsetting for us because we worked real hard. We had gotten used to the long hours. We always worked hard, served real good food, chatted with our customers, had a smile on our faces. Folk who were happy went away happy and came back again, over and over. We had many regular customers – at least half the folk who came by. They sure seemed happy to me.

But folk who were not happy would write a bad review.

That is why I am writing this. Those 2 bad reviews seemed to trigger others. This coincided with my wife getting cancer in her throat (yeh, she smoked). Work became even harder and money real tight because we had to pay somebody to replace my wife. I did everything I could to keep folk happy, but I reckon people are copy-cats because instead of praising the bits there were good, they complained about the bits that were bad.

I reckon I lost that business uniquely because of those reviews. People read reviews. One had written that my wife was rude, but that was not true. She was always sweet. Then another wrote that he'd had to wait half an hour to be served. That was a lie. Two of our regular families moved away. My wife was sick. Things took a downhill slide and once you start to slide downhill it sure is difficult to get back up again.

My wife died the following year, after we closed. I never told her we'd closed. It would have upset her. I work in a factory.

I wanted to write this because people need to know that what they write can do real damage. Real damage.

(name withheld).

Top tip! From Andree Brown, South Africa.

When making a chocolate cake add a tablespoon of malt vinegar to the mix. It brings out the chocolate flavour !

I don't have a recipe, but maybe some advice. As a child our family didn't have a medicine cabinet. If we were sick, in any form, my father made us chew on a clove or raw garlic. Your stomach will churn for thirty minutes and your breath will be awful, but you'll always get better.

From Lucas Kane

INTERNATIONAL FOOD

Celine Jacques, Switzerland

The French say their food is great,

I wonder why they do ?

It is just food upon a plate

No need for hullaballoo.

I've eaten well in Africa,

I've eaten well in Spain.

I've eaten rice with paprika

I've eaten wholesome grain.

A dish in Mexico is fine,

A cheese in Holland too.

Truly great Italian wine,

Or champagne from a shoe.

Croatian salad, vine from Greece,

German beer and Brussel sprout.

Good or bad I have to say

French food is really nowt.

Over the world I've spent

Meals with many men,

Cooks can be good, Heaven sent,

But the French think it's only them.

RONNY-RALF CHOCCIES

Claire Divall, Sussex

Depending on who you are and what you are like, this is either delicious or revolting! This is ideal party food, or even an unusual alternative for dessert at dinner.

- 2 average-sized milk chocolate bars
- 2 average-sized dark chocolate bars
- Half a tub of peanut butter
- 2 ozs. Butter
- A tablespoon of icing sugar
- Cake cases
- Melt the chocolate in a bain Marie. Place the cake cases on a bun tin or similar. Place a teaspoon of the melted chocolate in to the bottom of each cake case, and leave to chill in the fridge for an hour or so.
- In a bowl, mix the peanut butter, the butter and the icing sugar; you can put this over a little heat to help soften it. Add that to the chilled chocolate in the cake cases. Smooth it down and put in the fridge again, for a good hour.

"If this be magic, let it be an art lawful as eating."
— William Shakespeare

Did you know ... ? The South African word braii for a barbeque is from braii flaes, which means "burnt flesh" ?

... and while on that subject ...

Did you know ....? Our word barbeque comes from the French words "barbe" meaning beard, and "queue" meaning tail, and dates from when animals were roasted whole with the spike going in at the beard end and out at the tail end.

CB

THE BISTRO DEVIZES

thebistrodevizes.co.uk

The Story behind

Many years ago, before 'street food' became such a fashion, Peter Vaughan decided that on market days and busy Saturday and special festival days in the Wiltshire town of Devizes. Thinking about what would be easy to eat as a takeaway item plus what might be a bit different, he offered homemade falafels with homemade houmous and a seasonal salad in a toasted pitta bread with some homemade chilli jam.

At first some of the locals were puzzled, never having heard of falafels or eaten chickpeas before. However the taste was so good that they quickly 'caught on' and there would be queues of customers on the days when the steet food stall was out. Nowadays a meat based alternative is available but if ever peter dares to replace the falafels with some other choice , he will always get disappointed customers who were looking forward to some falafels.

The twist...

Peter has developed what he calls a 'naturally balanced' style of cuisine. Although classically trained, he wanted to learn more about food as fuel for our bodies and so studied nutrition and herbalism as well. All his dishes take into account the balance of nutrients as well as taste texture, flavour, look , seasonality and all the other things that make food good.

Chickpeas, as well as being very economical to use, are incredibly good for our health, in particular our hearts, plus they are a good source of protein. Falafels and houmous together in one 'hit' at lunchtime give you energy for the whole afternoon.

The main difference between Peter's falafels and a traditional recipe is that his are oven baked, rather than deep fried – much better for our systems but with no compromise on taste and texture.

The houmous recipe is also included. To cut down on fat, some of the oil is replaced with water but, once again, at no cost to flavour and texture.

THE BISTRO FALAFELS

Ingredients

- 1 Tbls rapeseed oil
- ¼ onion peeled and finely chopped
- 1 tsp ground coriander
- 1 tsp ground turmeric
- ½ tsp cayenne
- 1 225 tin chickpeas drained
- 1 garlic clove peeled and crushed
- 2 Tbls tahini
- 100g fresh bread crumbs
- Salt & pepper
- 1 egg beaten

Method

1. Heat oil in saucepan and saute onions until transparent (1-2 mins)
2. Add spices and cook out.
3. Add chickpeas, cook for 1 min then add crushed garlic and stir in.
4. Take off the heat and add tahini and breadcrumbs. Mash everything together with potato masher and season to taste.

5. Leave to cool slightly and then add beaten egg to bind everything together.
6. Use your hands to mould the mixture into little patties or balls.
7. Place on a greased baking tray and bake in the oven for approx. 20 mins
8. Serve warm topped with chilli jam/sauce

HOUMOUS

Ingredients

- 1 tin chickpeas
- 2 Tbls tahini
- juice 2 lemons
- ¼ tsp ground cumin
- ¼ tsp ground coriander
- pinch sea salt
- pinch cayenne
- 3 Tbls extra virgin olive oil
- 1 Tbls water

Method

1. Put everything into the food processor or a tall sided container if using a hand blender
2. Whizz up until correct consistency. If you need more liquid add either water or oil.
3. Taste to check balance. You may like to add more lemon juice (sour), or more tahini (bitter) or more salt. If you like chilli then you could add a bit more but don't overpower the chickpeas so go gently.
4. There are all sorts of things you can add to houmous – like fresh mint, crushed garlic, roasted peppers, sundried tomatoes – the list is endless but make sure that the flavor of what you add does overpower the true taste.

CB

HAPPY COOKING!

NUTRITIOUS SEEDED SPELT BREAD

Vaughan's Kitchen

vaughanskitchen.co.uk

The story behind

Spelt is an ancient relative of modern wheat and was brought to this country by the Romans. Legend has it that the Roman army called it their 'marching grain'. It is rich in nutrients with a higher level of protein, vitamins and minerals than our modern wheat, as well as being lower in gluten. It has a much more flavour, which has been described as "deliciously nutty and slightly sweet". So it tastes good AND it does you good. You will be bouncing with energy after eating it and it will keep the hunger pangs at bay for longer.

It has become very fashionable of late, possibly because of its superior(to modern wheat) flavour but it also is lower in gluten so people who find they have an intolerance to 'normal' wheat bread, find that spelt bread is easier on their digestive systems.

We use 50:50 in this recipe as the end result is lighter and so nearer to the texture or 'crumb' that we expect from our bread. However, you can easily use all spelt flour but made need to add an extra 25 mls of water, as the spelt flour may take up more liquid. Your dough should be soft and slightly sticky when you begin to knead.

The twist

We add molasses to this dough. Many recipes will add sugar, as this enhances the action of the yeast. White sugar contains no nutrients – these have been refined out of the finished product and molasses is a by-product of this process. It contains a high level of vitamins and minerals that were available before the processing began.

Adding to the mix will increase the nutritional level, increase the rise and give a really good taste to the finished product.

Seeds are also high in nutrition but in modern times we seem to use them very little. This is a way of giving your bread a lovely crunchy texture and increasing its nutritional benefits.

- 250 grams wholemeal spelt flour (can be wholegrain spelt)
- 250 grams strong white bread flour
- 1 teaspoon fast-action yeast (or 1 x 7g sachet)
- 2 teaspoons salt
- 2 tablespoons Rape Seed oil
- 1 tablespoon blackstrap molasses (not too generous or your dough will be too sticky)
- 300 mls water
- Assorted seeds to taste

1. Put flour, yeast, salt and oil into a large bowl and mix well.
2. Make well in centre. Add water, oil and molasses (it helps to oil or heat the spoon before you measure then it so that it doesn't stick). Bring dry ingredients into wet with dough scraper and mix thoroughly.
3. If at this stage the dough looks too dry, add more water but only 1 tablespoon at a time. The mix should be soft and elastic

4. Turn out on to work surface and knead the dough until smooth. If you dough is wet, avoid the temptation to throw

down lots of flour. Use the dough scraper to turn and roll it on the work surface, dust your hands with flour and then continue. If it begins to feel wet again, just repeat the process. It will come good and you will have a better 'crumb' from a wet dough than you will from a 'tight' or dry dough. This kneading this will take about 5 – 10 minutes. You can use an electric mixer with a dough hook

5. There are different styles of kneading so find what suits you. As long as the end result is a smooth dough with a good gluten structure your finished product will be fine.

6. Put back into scraped out bowl and cover with tea towel/bin liner /clingfilm and leave to double in size. The time this takes depends on the warmth of the place you put it in. You can even leave it in the fridge overnight for a long slow fermentation.

7. Knock back and flatten out into oblong shape. Scatter the desired amount of seeds onto 2/3rds of the dough. Fold over the empty third to 'catch' the seeds and then fold over again. Knead lightly until all seeds are incorporated.

8. Form into the final shape if free-form loaf or rolls or put into 500g/1lb loaf tin.

9. Leave to prove until doubled in size. Once again, the time it takes depends on the temperature. Allow 30 mins to 1 hour (unless putting in fridge as before – then it can be overnight)

10. Bake in a preheated oven at 200C/Gas mark 6

Cooking time: 500g loaf: 35 – 40mins; rolls 12-15 mins

"Food, the stoking-up process, the keeping alive of an individual flame, the process that begins before birth and is continued after it by the mother, and finally taken over by the individual himself, who goes on day after day putting an assortment of objects into a hole in his face without becoming surprised or bored."
— E.M. Forster

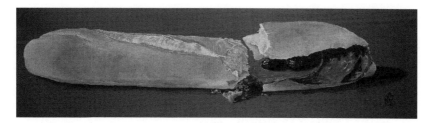

Mandy Broughton

AUBERGINE CRISPS

Nichola Rodgers, Tanzania, Africa

This is in memory of our cook, Joseph Afande, who died of cancer in Arusha. He was a talented and wonderful man.

- 3 aubergines
- 1 egg
- 4 ozs. Flour
- Salt and papper
- 6 cloves crushed garlic
- 2 teaspoons parmesan
- Half cup of milk
- A few spoons of oil

Slice the aubergines and put them in a dish. Sprinkle with salt and pepper. Place a heavy object on top in order to press out the slightly bitter juice aubergines have. Leave like that for 30 mins or so.

Wash the slices and pat dry with a cloth. Make a pancake mix using the other ingredients and dip each aubergine slice in. Fry quickly on each side and serve immediately. These "crisps" will go soggy f left for more than 20 – 30 mins.

ICELANDIC APPLE CRUMBLE

From Anja Eriksson, Reykjavik

- Cooking apples – 3 or 4 of them
- Walnuts – a teacup or so
- Sultanas or raisins – about half a cup
- Half a cup of water
- Brown sugar – about 2 tablespoons
- Porridge oats
- 1 weetabix or similar
- About 5 ozs. Of marg or butter

Butter an oven dish thoroughly and light the oven full blast. Chop the apples up in to fairly small pieces and put them, with the raisins and the walnuts, in to the dish. Crumble (use your fingers) the butter, Weetabix, sugar and oats till it is well mixed and then pour over the apples mixture, covering it totally. This is important because the raisins will burn and go hard if they are not properly covered.

Place in oven and immediately turn it down to around 130 degrees. Bake for 40 minutes. Serve piping hot with cream.

Mandy Broughton

You don't need a silver fork to eat good food.

-   Paul Prudhomme

FOOD SPOILAGE CHART

Olav Forsgren, Sweden

The gag test

Anything that makes you gag is spoiled (except for leftovers from what you cooked for yourself last night).

Eggs

When something starts pecking its way out of the shell, the egg is probably past its prime.

Meat

If opening the refrigerator door causes stray animals from a three-block radius to congregate outside your house, the meat is spoiled.

Canned goods

Any canned goods that have become the size or shape of a basketball should be disposed of. Carefully.

Wine

It should not taste like salad dressing.

Potatoes

Fresh potatoes do not have roots, branches, or dense, leafy undergrowth.

General rule of thumb

Most food cannot be kept longer than the average life span of a hamster. Keep a hamster in your refrigerator to gauge this.

Also from Olav:

A businessman had arranged an important formal dinner party at his home where they were going to serve stuffed whole baked fish as the main course. While the guests were eating the appetizer, the cook came to the host and whispered: "Please come urgently to the kitchen."

The host went to the kitchen where the cook explained that while she was serving the starter, the cat ate a big chunk of the fish which they were going to serve. The host said, "Just fill the hole with stuffing and turn the other side up, nobody will notice."

The fish was served and when they were nearly finished eating, the host was again called to the kitchen. The cook said, "The cat is dead!"

The host rushed back to the dinner party and apologized, "Something was wrong with the fish and everyone must have their stomachs pumped out at the hospital."

When they came back everything was still fine and the host went to ask the cook, "Where is the cat?"

"Oh," said the chef, "The cat is still by the road where the truck ran it down!"

"So long as you have food in *your mouth you have solved all questions for the time being.*"

\- *Franz Kafka*

QUICK NUT ROAST/VEGGIE BURGERS/STUFFING

Lucy Thorburn, France

Ingredients

- 1 medium tin white beans/ black eyed peas or similar
- 1 tin cooked chestnuts
- 240 g cashew nuts
- 2 onions
- 2 cloves garlic
- 1 veggie stock cube
- dash sherry [optional]
- 1 teaspoon mustard
- 1 teaspoon harrisa paste [optional]
- 1 large egg/ 2 small eggs
- salt/pepper to taste

Method

- chop onions and garlic finely and fry until transparent
- chop nuts finely
- mix ingredients together and mash with spud masher or similar

- beat egg and add to mix, fold in

- add seasoning

- grease and line large loaf tin or oven proof dish

- place in medium oven for half an hour or until surface is browned.

- To make burgers, simply form into shape, dust with flour and fry.

- Serve with gravy, cranberry sauce or chutney

-

NICHTS ESSEN!
From Lucy Thorburn

I met the love of my life when he was about to emerge from his 25 year army career, hence our first holiday together was in the army ski lodge in Southern Germany. This is where I discovered the easy way to lose a huge amount of weight in just three weeks - German cuisine! If you like fresh veg., fruit, fish and salad, take sandwiches! We were mountain walking and canoeing, both hunger-inducing activities.

 John talked endlessly about the wonderful restaurant at the summit of this or that mountain. Shunning the moving chair lift on the grounds that it was Summer and falling from a great height onto rocks is a different kettle of fish from falling onto deep snow, I ascended the hard way. Arriving at the summit, there was a delightful traditional restaurant with a terrace overlooking the valley below. I was so hungry, I could have eaten a scabby horse. I ordered a 'hunters' plate' [I think!]. When it arrived, it was pickled something [might have once been cabbage, but was sadly in need of a decent funeral], spuds which had been boiled [but not that day] and maybe put in a jar, and something which might have been meat in some kind of sauce. I couldn't eat it. This set the pattern for the following three weeks. Even the cakes, for which Germany is legendary, were damp and filled with 'squirty' cream.

John took pity on me one morning, in between complaints about paying for so many meals I had refused. My jeans were so loose by then I didn't have to undo them to take them off. We had a microwave in our digs and he promised me boiled eggs for breakfast. I was in the shower when he embarked on this culinary feast. Strangely, so was the microwave - well, not in the shower, but on an adjacent shelf. He knew that eggs have a tendency to explode in microwaves, so he prevented this by sitting them in cups full of water. The next thing I knew, the door blew off the microwave in an unexpectedly impressive explosion,eggs, cups, boiling water-I was scared out of my wits!

John tried to persuade me that the standard of cuisine in Germany had gone downhill due to the wall coming down and the place being full of East Germans, but I know better.

A German friend in U.K., horrified at my rejection of her native cuisine, invited us round for a meal. I told her I didn't eat meat [I wasn't falling for that one again]. All should have been well. I watched her put water and flour into a pressing machine to make some kind of worms - a very poor relation of pasta[?] and she kindly put some herring under the grill for me. They should have been really tasty, if only a friend hadn't phoned from Germany, with an ensuing conversation culminating in the fire alarm going off and cinders for dinner. A bit like my childhood.

My mother was sometimes confused and I will always remember the Sunday when the joint remained on the doorstep and she roasted a pair of shoes - putting the spuds round them, basting and everything. If you have seen the black and white film 'The gold rush', you will be able to visualise the ensuing meal.

I have had some weird experiences with food, an expedition to Belize where the food fund went mysteriously astray and we only had tins rejected and abandoned by the British army, God bless their little cotton socks and survived on mostly coconut. We had competitions to develop the most efficient way to open the wretched things [there isn't much to amuse one in Belize when the daily dives and logs were complete].

There was also the diving trip in the Dardenelles where we were on board ship [I use that word lightly - it was sinking lower and lower in the water each day due to a rather large hole in the stern], for a week. They started off well, buying sufficient baguettes for the whole trip the day before we left. The evening meal on the first night was soup[?] made with chicken knuckles. We thought this was a starter, but no, that was it! We had to stage a mutiny [yes, really!] in order to be put ashore a couple of days later to access restaurants.

I live in France and some of the local dishes don't tempt me, however the food can be sublime. I love Egyptian and Lebanese food and find Morrocan yummy stuff to die for, but German food - nein danke!

"If you can't feed 100 people, just feed one."

-   Mother Teresa

Food and cancer

From Lucy Thorburn.

http://mybreastcancertreatmentinfrance.blogspot.co.uk/

About two months before I found out I had breast cancer we were invited to dinner with friends who were doing a 'raclette' evening. This is what I [privately] call 'boy scout food', because there is a communal hot plate thingie where you cook your own meat. There was also a large selection of cheeses on offer. About ten minutes into the meal I made a sharp exit to the loo as my body had decided, without warning, that meat and cheese were no longer on the menu. Later it turned violently against eggs. I found the problem with cheese lay with rennet - the substance used to make cheese hard. Believe it or not, I had no problem with Roquefort or other blue cheeses, or soft cheese. I would have thought the pong of the blues would have put me off, but I could handle the very smelliest of goat cheeses!

I went through phases with eating - at first I was crazy for avacados which, according to the internet, have some active anti-cancer properties. Now I can't face them.

It is difficult to follow a 'balanced diet' when chemo makes you feel so wretched and I know that ,in the week before the next session, I eat like a bear preparing for Winter. I was overweight when I started chemo, and, so far, despite my best efforts, I have lost 8 kilos. I still have a way to go before I am thin - I'm a size 12 - but 'they' say it is important to keep your weight up. Most days, apart from when I am doing 'duvet time', I force myself to do 2/3 k's a day walking the dog. I have a theory that it pumps the poison round and boosts the old immune system. The Oncologist is keen on you joining a gym. Oh yeah, you have that filthy muck pumped round your system and go and spend an afternoon doing airobics. I think not. It might not be so bad here because they have special classes for us baldies. I just couldn't 'do' the loud music and being shouted at for being an uncoordinated tosspot. She let me off when I promised to walk a lot.

I have to tell you that my partner has changed into an angel during this whole business. When 'they' put me on Taxoter and I hadn't eaten for six days, I woke up at 2 a.m. starving hungry but couldn't work out what I could eat. At 3 a.m. I meekly asked if he would consider going downstairs and heating up a packet of Thai soup. See- spices again! I managed some of this, finishing the lot eventually, eating a whole [small] melon for my next meal. Maybe this is a 'balanced diet' for a crazy chemo person?????

In France you are given an immune system booster jab the day after chemo. I don't know whether it is that, or the anti-nausea meds which act like quick drying cement in the gut. Whatever you do, don't get constipated. I have a friend who was hospitalized because of this. I avoided this side effect by forcing myself to eat at least two prunes and two figs a day, along with live yoghurt.

Late into my series of chemo sessions, when I still have no real appetite, breakfast consists of Greek yoghurt and honey. I can't eat bread - my favourite food - it gives me horrible indigestion. Flat coke helps with this, but I had to resort to asking for a script for Omeprazole. I take a full dose [20mg] the day after chemo and half a dose for the two following days. I could take more, maybe I should take more and make life easier, but I hate taking pills. I don't find over-the-counter meds help at all.

Bananas are a staple and I eat dried apricots because I think they are high in iron. Weirdly I have found I can eat fish if it is cooked somewhere else [my sense of smell is acute at the moment]. Today I had a sea bass stuffed with limes and garlic looking out over the sea. I refused the rice/chips which went with, but the fish was wonderful. Some days I can even manage French fish and chips - the batter is very light here.

 The message is 'eat what you fancy', however the weird thing which saved my life in the early weeks/ months was chai. Chai, an Indian tea loaded with ginger, cardamon, tumeric, pepper e.t.c. [all of which are on the 'magical against cancer' list of things to eat/drink], with hot milk and honey. I know it probably sounds disgusting but I couldn't stomach anything else at first. I am surprised how I crave ginger. I have exhausted the local supply of lemon and ginger tea and all those crossing the Channel have to pay a l+g t toll!

"If God didn't intend us to eat animals,
then why did he make them out of meat?"

- John Cleese

HOW TO COOK FOOD FROM A PACKET:

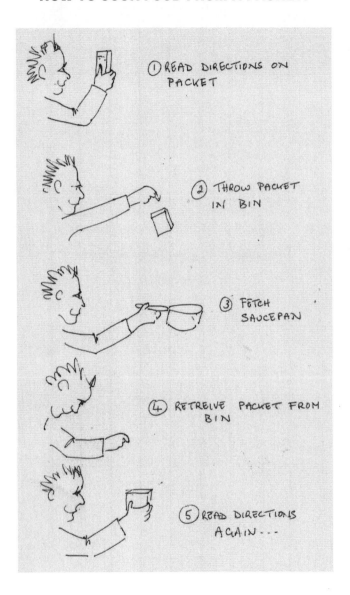

1. READ DIRECTIONS ON PACKET
2. THROW PACKET IN BIN
3. FETCH SAUCEPAN
4. RETREIVE PACKET FROM BIN
5. READ DIRECTIONS AGAIN...

"You can tell a lot about a fellow's character

by his way of eating jelly beans."

- Ronald Reagan

CHICKEN CARMEN

Victor Rudez, Croatia

In the 1970s there was a couturière named Franka, Baroness Von Holstein. She was a friend of Victor's, based in Knightsbridge, London. Among Franka's many clients was the actress Ava Gardner. Ava had a maid from Portugal by the name of Carmen, and she cooked this chicken dish when there were guests for dinner.

- Chicken drumsticks – 2 or 3 per person

- Seasoned flour – enough to cover the drumsticks properly

- Fresh chopped tarragon – about 1 tablespoon per person

- Dried tarragon – about ¼ Tbsp. per person

- Olive oil for frying

Use a non-stick pan. Roll the drum sticks in the seasoned flour and the dried tarragon. If the drum sticks are slightly damp, the flour mixture will stick more easily. Heat the oil up in a pan, and put the chicken in to cook. Cook on a low heat turning regularly, and sprinkling fresh tarragon on regularly. You can put a lid on to help it cook more quickly, but be careful the flour "crust" doesn't go soggy. It takes around 40 minutes to cook.

Serve with almost anything. It is delicious with rice, salad, and mushrooms fried in garlic. Best eaten piping hot.

THE TOTALLY EXCELLENT PHOTO CLUB FRUIT CAKE

Catherine Broughton

I call this cake the Photo Club Fruit Cake because I bake one every week for my husband to take with him to his photography group:-

Put the oven on to full heat.

Take three large eggs and weigh them. They will probably way around 200 g. Whatever the weight, measure the same again in self-raising flour, marg and/or butter, and brown sugar.

Mix the sugar and marg together until it is creamy. Add the eggs. Beat until thoroughly mixed. Place the flour in the large bowl, and add as many glacé cherries, walnuts, almonds, mixed nuts, raisins, sultanas and other dried or glacé fruit as you wish. The weight of the fruit and nuts doesn't matter as long as they are all thoroughly covered in flour. If you don't cover them in flour first they will simply sink to the bottom of the cake as it is cooking. Mix the flour with the fruit and nuts in to the eggy mixture. You can add a large spoonful of marmalade if you have some. Mix slowly with big circular movements, allowing air to get in.

When you place this in the oven, in a thoroughly greased cake tin, immediately turn the heat down to approximately 140, gas 4. Cook for approximately 1 hour and 10 mins. Test with a knife. For best results remove from oven when the knife is still slightly sticky. Once cooked remove immediately from the oven otherwise it will dry out. It can cool in its tin.

Jenni Gayle

Interviews

MARY HOLBROOK, ARTIST

Q1. Tell us a bit about you, where you are from and where you live.

I was born and raised in California, U.S.A., but am currently living in Bilbao, Spain and am planning on permanently moving in a few months to Nicaragua.

Q2. Tell us about the medium you use for your art work, what started you, what you love.

I tend to like to make pencil or pen sketches, or watercolour. I enjoy acrylics, but don't use them as often. I kind of just naturally got into art...as a child I was always using the binder paper that my mom gave me for school to doodle or draw/sketch whatever came to my mind, and I finally started taking art classes at school.

Q3. Tell us about your other interests and hobbies.

Other interests and hobbies? Well, I have my TEFL Certificate from the International TEFL Academy to teach English as a foreign language, which is why I am currently in Spain, and am planning on moving to Nicaragua. I love working with people from different cultures which is one of the reasons I chose my career, and I absolutely love to travel to see the world! I especially love working with kids, and plan on teaching English with kids in Nicaragua at the local elementary school in the community where I stayed almost 2 years ago.

Q4. You are a great traveller. Which foods do you prefer to cook and eat?

Foods...hmmm...In Nicaragua I got very used to gallo pinto (a mix of rice and beans) and tortillas and fried bananas (the Latin side of me came out when I went there, and now in Spain I have a lot of Spanish tortillas, and since I live with a Venezuelan couple here, we have arepas every week, and I love them! I don't really have one food that I prefer over another. I like to vary my food variety and just try all sorts of new foods that seem to strike my fancy:)

Q5. Have you ever had any particularly dreadful experiences with food abroad?

The only bad food experience I ever had was when they killed the pig of the community in Nicaragua for someone's birthday dinner, and we have to eat all the gross parts, like the ears and all...ugh!

Q6. Or any particularly good experiences?

Everything else was a good experience, except that I hate avocados and sushi.

Q7. Which countries have you visited?

When I was little I visited Montreal/Quebec in Canada for a week or two. The almost two years ago I went to Nicaragua. I live to say I lived there, because I was living just like the locals for a full 6 weeks, being completely immersed in their language and culture. I visited Nicaragua again a year ago for a week during Easter break with a high school group.

Q8. Which countries have you lived in?

Places I've lived...California almost my whole life, of course. Then Nicaragua for 6 weeks, and now I am living in Bilbao, Spain

Q9. do you tend to travel in comfort or do you go the cheapest possible - or a mix of the two.

I tend to mix comfort with cheap, but mainly because for me comfortable is usually cheap. I loved the way I lived in Nicaragua in my little dirt house, and it was the cheapest way to live! I like to live with as little as I can. For me it feels very satisfying knowing that the world won't end if you don't live in a house with Wi-Fi!

Q10. tell us something surprising about you!

Something surprising: I was happier living in a dirt house with no running water, and limited electricity than I ever felt my whole life living with plenty of running water, hot baths, electricity, technology and all, in my big, two-part, two story white house! :)

If you would like to check out my Instagram, I have some of my pictures of the places I have been, and I am always posting more and more:

instagram.com/meholbrook96

facebook.com/meholbrook96

Mandy Broughton

DANIEL HARRINGTON, RESTAURANT OWNER

The Smokehouse, Uckfield

Q1. Tell us a bit about you your restaurant and why you started the business

We came to Uckfield to turn around a beautiful old building and bring some life back to her again by serving American style food and beverages.

Q2. Tell us about the type of food and drink if you prefer to serve. Do you have any specialities?

We have 3 big sellers at the moment...

Paprika Nachos with salsa, guacamole and jalapeños and melted Cheese.

The Whammy Burger , Angus Beef, cheese, Sloppy Joes all stacked within our Brioche Buns served with Chips salad and Cajun Onion Rings.

Finally our Full Rack of Ribs with a juicy Bourbon Glaze and Corn on Cob and Sweet Potato Chips.

Q3. what was the most difficult part of setting up a restaurant? And the most fun ?

It was tricky how everything came together at the last minute, plenty of sleepless nights and long days.

The best part was seeing the vision you have in your head finally in front of you.

Q4. Have you had any particularly difficult customers?

Most have enjoyed the ideas and what we are aiming to achieve, the biggest criticism I've had is changing the name from Maidens Head, but sadly we are something different to what it was before and needed to state and send that message with a change in name.

Q5. Do you enjoy cooking yourself or do you prefer to use the cook?

The menu itself I have written and was completely my ideas and has been a labour of love for the pass 2 years.

Q6. Are there any foods or drinks you absolutely loathe?

I'm a bit against an English roast, although I make a mean one 15 years of being a chef in the industry and for some reason the roast represents working on a Sunday !!

Q7. Tell us about any particularly horrible experience you have had, or funny experience, with food - anywhere in the world

Probably my worst experience from a chef perspective was not realising my commis chef had made our cheesecake using salt instead of sugar and serving to a wedding party did not go down to well .... Many years ago now !!

Q8. Would you say that the rules and regulations relating to hygiene in restaurants in the UK are about right?

I think they are necessary and need to be adhered to as most is just common sense when working with food which I always have felt if I went to a restaurant I would want the chef to work clean and organised and respect and care for the dish they are preparing.

Q9. Have you spent much time in other countries? Where?

Only on holiday and sadly these have dried up recently and for the time being as the job takes over the life. But hoping when everything eventually settles down I may get to take my family away this year.

Q10. Tell us something surprising about you!

Surprising is staying on my feet all day when I have a metal femur after a car crash ten years ago and running up and down the stairs.

ATLA Publishing
atlapublishing.com

16565825R00111

Printed in Great Britain
by Amazon